John Flavel

John Flavel (1627–1691)

Engraving from an original picture
in Dr. Williams's Library

"An Honest, Well Experienced Heart"

The Piety of John Flavel

Introduced and Edited by
Adam Embry

Reformation Heritage Books
Grand Rapids, Michigan

Reformation Heritage Books
2965 Leonard St. NE
Grand Rapids, MI 49525
616-977-0889 / Fax 616-285-3246
orders@heritagebooks.org
www.heritagebooks.org

Printed in the United States of America
12 13 14 15 16 17/10 9 8 7 6 5 4 3 2 1

Library of Congress Cataloging-in-Publication Data

Flavel, John, 1630?-1691.
  "An honest, well experienced heart" : the piety of John Flavel / introduced and edited by Adam Embry.
      p. cm. — (Profiles in Reformed spirituality)
  Includes bibliographical references.
  ISBN 978-1-60178-183-3 (pbk. : alk. paper) 1. Piety. 2. Puritans—England—Doctrines. I. Embry, Adam. II. Title.
  BV4647.P5F53 2012
  248.4'852—dc23
                                                    2012021427

To my wife,

**Charlotte,
and our children,**

for their love and support

PROFILES IN REFORMED SPIRITUALITY
series editors—Joel R. Beeke and Michael A. G. Haykin

Table of Contents

Section Three: Seasons of the Heart

Section Four: Discerning the Heart

Conclusion

Profiles in Reformed Spirituality

Charles Dickens's famous line in *A Tale of Two Cities*—
"It was the best of times, it was the worst of times"
—seems well suited to western evangelicalism since
the 1960s. On the one hand, these decades have seen
much for which to praise God and to rejoice. In His
goodness and grace, for instance, Reformed truth is
no longer a house under siege. Growing numbers
identify themselves theologically with what we hold
to be biblical truth, namely, Reformed theology and
piety. And yet, as an increasing number of Reformed
authors have noted, there are many sectors of the
surrounding western evangelicalism that are charac-
terized by great shallowness and a trivialization of the
weighty things of God. So much of evangelical worship seems barren. And when it comes to spirituality,
there is little evidence of the riches of our heritage as
Reformed evangelicals.

As it was at the time of the Reformation, when the
watchword was *ad fontes*—"back to the sources"—so
it is now: The way forward is backward. We need to
go back to the spiritual heritage of Reformed evangelicalism to find the pathway forward. We cannot live
in the past; to attempt to do so would be antiquarian-
ism. But our Reformed forebearers in the faith can
teach us much about Christianity, its doctrines, its
passions, and its fruit.

And they can serve as our role models. As R. C. Sproul has noted of such giants as Augustine, Martin Luther, John Calvin, and Jonathan Edwards: "These men all were conquered, overwhelmed, and spiritually intoxicated by their vision of the holiness of God. Their minds and imaginations were captured by the majesty of God the Father. Each of them possessed a profound affection for the sweetness and excellence of Christ. There was in each of them a singular and unswerving loyalty to Christ that spoke of a citizenship in heaven that was always more precious to them than the applause of men."[1]

To be sure, we would not dream of placing these men and their writings alongside the Word of God. John Jewel (1522–1571), the Anglican apologist, once stated: "What say we of the fathers, Augustine, Ambrose, Jerome, Cyprian?... They were learned men, and learned fathers; the instruments of the mercy of God, and vessels full of grace. We despise them not, we read them, we reverence them, and give thanks unto God for them. Yet...we may not make them the foundation and warrant of our conscience: we may not put our trust in them. Our trust is in the name of the Lord."[2]

Seeking, then, both to honor the past and yet not idolize it, we are issuing these books in the series Profiles in Reformed Spirituality. The design is to introduce the spirituality and piety of the Reformed

---

1. R. C. Sproul, "An Invaluable Heritage," *Tabletalk* 23, no. 10 (October 1999): 5–6.

2. Cited in Barrington R. White, "Why Bother with History?" *Baptist History and Heritage* 4, no. 2 (July 1969): 85.

tradition by presenting descriptions of the lives of notable Christians with select passages from their works. This combination of biographical sketches and collected portions from primary sources gives a taste of the subjects' contributions to our spiritual heritage and some direction as to how the reader can find further edification through their works. It is the hope of the publishers that this series will provide riches for those areas where we are poor and light of day where we are stumbling in the deepening twilight.

—Joel R. Beeke
Michael A. G. Haykin

Acknowledgments

In my 1813 edition of Flavel's *Keeping the Heart*, the professors of Andover Theological Seminary wrote, "The works of the Rev. John Flavel have been greatly useful to the church of Christ in England and America.... It is appropriate to the present season of coldness and indifference on the part of many professors of religion and contains much that is important to all classes of Christians." That two-hundred-year-old statement agrees with the purposes behind the Reformation Heritage Books Profiles in Reformed Spirituality series. For this reason, I extend gratitude to Dr. Joel Beeke and Dr. Michael Haykin, the series editors of this book, for including John Flavel in the series. Dr. Beeke's and Dr. Haykin's writings on church history and biblical spirituality have helped me love Christ more. I am also thankful for the labors of the team at Reformation Heritage Books, Jay Collier and Annette Gysen. Both were efficient and encouraging in seeing this book to print.

A group of Puritan and Flavel students also deserve my appreciation. Dr. Stephen Yuille graciously reviewed the introduction. He has written on Flavel, among other Puritans, and his writings are worth your time reading. I've enjoyed beneficial conversations with Brian Cosby and Nathan Parker, both doctoral students studying Flavel. Expect to see excellent pastoral scholarship on Flavel from them in the future. My supervisor and friend at The Southern Baptist Theological Seminary, Dr. Shawn Wright, deserves my thanks for first teaching me Puritan history and theology.

The church I serve, Auburndale Baptist, deserves my appreciation for their willingness to hear so many Flavel quotes in my sermons! This is a church that has furnished my office wall with a portrait of Flavel and my bookshelf with a 1700 edition of Flavel's *Fountain of Life*. I am truly a blessed pastor to serve such a loving and thoughtful people.

My parents purchased a copy of *The Works of John Flavel* for my seminary education. Those volumes have given me instruction in godliness and pastoral ministry, so I am also indebted to John Flavel and his ministry.

I am most thankful for my wife, Charlotte Ann, and her encouragement as I have learned theology and pastoral ministry from Flavel. She has been patient with me as I have read and studied Flavel for the past few years. She is to me "a good wife being… the best companion…the fittest and readiest assistant in work…and the greatest grace and honor that can be, to him that hath her."[1]

Adam Embry
Louisville, Kentucky

---

1. Thomas Gataker, *A Good Wife God's Gift* (London, 1637), 166.

Note of interest: The engraving at the end of most selections is attributed to Sir Walter Raleigh's *The Sea-Mans Triumph, Declaring the Honorable Actions of Such Gentlemen Captains and Sailors...Lately Brought to Dartmouth* (London, 1592).

I could say much, though not enough, of the excellency of his preaching; of his seasonable, suitable and spiritual matter; of his plain expositions of scripture, his taking method, his genuine and natural deductions, his convincing arguments, his clear and powerful demonstrations, his heart-searching applications, and his comfortable supports to those that were afflicted in conscience. In short that person must have a very soft head, or a very hard heart, or both, that could sit under his ministry unaffected.

—A church member under Flavel's ministry

John Flavel

The Piety of John Flavel
(1627–1691)

Early in the 1670s, a gentleman entered Mr. Boulter's London bookshop in search of literary plays. Having none in inventory, Boulter seized the opportunity to show him a theological work titled *Keeping the Heart*.[1] Examining the title, the gentleman exclaimed, "What a damnable fanatic was he who made this book!" He mockingly offered to buy it, if only to burn it. Boulter stood undeterred by his recommendation. Reluctantly, the gentleman finally promised to read it. A month later, he returned to the bookshop in a far more somber mood, admitting to Boulter, "Sir, I most heartily thank you for putting this book into my hand; I bless God that moved you to do it, it hath

---

1. This book is also titled *A Saint Indeed; or, The Great Work of a Christian Explained and Pressed from Proverbs 4:23* (London, 1671). "Keep thy heart with all diligence; for out of it are the issues of life" (Prov. 4:23). This work was first published in 1668. Later reprints came out of London in 1670, 1671, 1673, 1675, 1677, 1680, 1682, 1684, 1689, 1698, 1701, 1729, 1768, and 1796. Flavel's book was published at Edinburgh in 1696 and 1789, Belfast in 1743, Glasgow in 1754, and Mullingar in 1799. In the American colonies, the book was published in 1726 (Boston); 1795 (Amherst, N.H.); 1801 (New Brunswick, N.J.); 1813 and 1815 (Boston); 1817 (Hartford, Conn.), and 1819 (Boston). The numerous republications of *A Saint Indeed / Keeping the Heart* show its spiritual usefulness throughout Old and New England.

saved my soul; blessed be God that ever I came into your shop." He then purchased a hundred copies to distribute among the poor.[2]

Who wrote this life-changing book? The author was John Flavel. Born at Worcestershire in 1627, Flavel was part of a family steeped in Puritan piety.[3] In later years, he affectionately remembered his father, Richard, as "one that was inwardly acquainted with God; and being full of bowels to his children often carried them before the Lord, prayed and pleaded with God for them, wept and made supplications for them."[4] Flavel initially had little interest in Christianity, despite this godly upbringing. "I was carried away," he remembered, "so many years in the course

---

2. "Thus it pleased God to bless the sermons, discourses and writings of Mr. Flavel." *The Life of the Late Rev. Mr. John Flavel, Minister of Dartmouth*, in *The Works of John Flavel* (Edinburgh: Banner of Truth, 1997), 1:xiv. No author is named for Flavel's *Memoir* in his works; however, John Quick is the author of the memoir. Quick's *Icones Sacrae Anglicanae* contains a biographical sketch of Flavel similar to the one contained in Flavel's works. "The only extant biography of any appreciable length is by John Quick." See Kwai Sing Chang, "John Flavel of Dartmouth, 1630–1691" (PhD diss., University of Edinburgh, 1952).

3. According to Flavel, godly families are "of special consideration, both as to our temporal and eternal good: For whether the families in which we grow up were great or small in Israel; whether our parents were of a higher or lower class and rank among men, yet if they were such as feared God, and wrought righteousness, if they took any care to educate you righteously, and trained you up 'in the nurture and admonition of the Lord,' you are bound to reckon it among your chief mercies." *Divine Conduct; or, The Mystery of Providence: A Treatise upon Psalm 57:2*, in *The Works of John Flavel* (Edinburgh: Banner of Truth, 1997), 4:370.

4. John Flavel, *The Fountain of Life: A Display of Christ in His Essential and Mediatorial Glory: 42 Sermons*, in *The Works of John Flavel* (Edinburgh: Banner of Truth, 1997), 1:257.

of this world.... I studied to know many other things, but I knew not myself."[5] Yet, at some point during Flavel's youth, the Holy Spirit led him to Christ. Flavel describes this transformation as follows:

My body which is but the garment of my soul, I kept and nourished with excessive care, but my soul was long forgotten, and had been lost for ever, as others daily are, had not God roused it, by the convictions of his Spirit, out of that deep oblivion and deadly slumber. When the God that formed it, out of free grace to the work of his own hands, had thus recovered it to a sense of its own worth and danger, my next work was to get it united with Christ, and thereby secured from the wrath to come.[6]

Flavel completed grammar school and followed in his brother Phineas's footsteps, enrolling at Oxford University, where he excelled at his studies. Upon graduation in 1650, he accepted the position of assistant minister at a church in Diptford, Devon. The minister died a short time later, so Flavel assumed full responsibility of the ministry. He possessed a clear appreciation for his pastoral duties: "The scope and end of the ministry is for the church's benefit and advantage."[7] He also desired to know the spiritual state of his flock, stating, "A prudent minister will study the souls of his people, more than the best

---

5. John Flavel, *Pneumatologia: A Treatise of the Soul of Man*, in *The Works of John Flavel* (Edinburgh: Banner of Truth, 1997), 2:483.

6. Flavel, *Treatise of the Soul of Man*, 2:483–84.

7. John Flavel, *Husbandry Spiritualized: The Heavenly Use of Earthly Things*, in *The Works of John Flavel* (Edinburgh: Banner of Truth, 1997), 5:21.

human books in his library; and not choose what is easiest for him, but what is most necessary for them."[8] In addition, Flavel understood his own need for spiritual growth as a pastor, often saying, "All our reading, studying, and preaching, is but trifling hypocrisy, till the things read, studied, and preached, be felt in some degree upon our own hearts."[9]

Ministry in Dartmouth

In 1656, Flavel moved to the southwest seaport town of Dartmouth,[10] where he assisted Allan Geare at St. Savior's and St. Clement's, preaching on Sundays and lecturing on Wednesdays.[11] Six years later, in 1662, the Church of England imposed the Clarendon Code, which restricted nonconformist activity among civil rulers, laypeople, and church ministers.

---

8. John Flavel, *The Character of a Complete Evangelical Pastor, Drawn by Christ*, in *The Works of John Flavel* (Edinburgh: Banner of Truth, 1997), 6:571.

9. Flavel, *Complete Evangelical Pastor*, 6:568. It was known that "being assiduous in reading, meditation and prayer, he increased in ministerial knowledge daily so that he attained to a high degree of eminency and reputation for his useful labours in the church." *Life of Flavel*, 1:iv.

10. The church at Dartmouth had considered John Howe as a possible pastor. However, he became one of Oliver Cromwell's chaplains and later ministered in the Great Torrington church. Edward Windeatt, "John Flavell: A Notable Dartmouth Puritan and His Bibliography," in *Transactions of the Devonshire Association for the Advancement of Science, Literature, and Art* 43 (1911): 3–5.

11. Prior to this move, Flavel's wife, Joan Randall, died while giving birth in 1655, and the child died as well. Flavel later married Elizabeth Stapell, who died around 1672. Soon after, he married Agnes Downes, who passed away around 1684. Finally, Flavel married Dorothy Jefferies. *Oxford Dictionary of National Biography*, s.v. "Flavell, John."

St. Savior's Church, Dartmouth

As a result, both Geare and Flavel were ejected from the church. Neither this nor Geare's sudden death discouraged Flavel from continuing to minister to his people. He supplemented his income by teaching at a Latin school along with a fellow minister, James Burdwood, who later published a sermon from Flavel on how Christians test their hearts for signs of godliness.[12] This ministry continued for three years, until 1665 and the enforcement of the Five Mile Act. As the name suggests, this act required nonconformist ministers to stay five miles away from their churches. As a result, Flavel moved to nearby Slapton. Still, he remained devoted to his people, visiting them whenever possible and producing a number of books for their spiritual benefit.[13]

These years were exceedingly difficult for nonconformist ministers. The vast majority of them, however, remained committed to preaching the gospel and cultivating godliness among their people. As John Coffey observes, "Instead of fleeing...dissenters generally chose to stay put and face up to persecution. The longing for a theocracy had been displaced by a sense that tribulation was the lot of the godly."[14] That is certainly true of Flavel. According to the earliest biographical account of his life, "he

---

12. Windeatt, "John Flavell," 7. See selection 44.

13. Around this time, he wrote *Navigation Spiritualized* and *Husbandry Spiritualized*. These works spiritualize sailing and farming. This is a common genre among the Puritans, but as Dewey Wallace remarks, "The master at the art of spiritualizing the creatures...was John Flavel." *The Spirituality of the Later English Puritans: An Anthology* (Macon, Ga.: Mercer University, 1987), xxx.

14. John Coffey, *Persecution and Toleration in Protestant England, 1558–1689* (Essex: Pearson Education, 2000), 177.

thought the souls of his flock to be more precious than to be so tamely neglected. He took all opportunities of ministering the Word and Sacraments to them in private meetings, and joined with other ministers in solemn days of fasting and humiliation, to pray that God would once more restore the ark of his covenant unto his afflicted Israel."[15] Flavel recognized the value of a persecuted ministry. He was convinced that God used it to sanctify him, thus making him a more effective pastor—better able to minister to his people. He explains:

> When we could not preach the doctrine of faith, we were reduced, by a blessed necessity, to live the life of faith. The rules of patience, humility, and satisfaction in the will of God, were wont to prescribe from our pulpits to the people, we were necessitated to practice and apply to ourselves in our sad solitudes, and various distresses, through which the Lord hath led us. So that now we come better furnished to the work, than ever before.[16]

Imprisonment was a constant threat for nonconformists. Flavel's parents were imprisoned at Newgate in 1665, where they caught the plague and died upon their release.[17] The risk of arrest followed Flavel and those who met secretly to hear him preach at Barnstaple and Chittlehampton or on the rocks at low tide at the Kingbridge estuary. On one occasion, Flavel disguised himself as a woman to travel

---

15. *Life of Flavel*, 1:vi.

16. Flavel, *Complete Evangelical Pastor*, 6:584–85.

17. *Life of Flavel*, 1:iv.

undetected to Totnes, where he performed a baptism. On another occasion, he rode his horse into the ocean at Slapton Sands to elude the police. He escaped arrest at a ministerial prayer meeting in London, although his friend and fellow minister, William Jenkyn, was not so fortunate.[18] A respite from persecution finally arrived in 1672, when Charles II issued an indulgence, allowing licensed nonconformist ministers to preach. Along with 163 members of his congregation, Flavel sent a letter to the king, thanking him for religious toleration.[19] Flavel continued to preach and write throughout the remainder of the decade. In the 1680s, however, persecution resumed and intensified.[20] Eventually, he was placed under house arrest. As always, he used his circumstances to his pastoral advantage, again publishing his sermons for the benefit of his people.[21]

In 1687, James II issued a Declaration of Indulgence, which nullified all laws and penalties against the nonconformists and permitted them to worship publicly. Within two years, William and Mary ascended the throne and passed the Act of Toleration, which guaranteed religious freedom to

---

18. *Life of Flavel*, 1:ix.

19. G. Lyon Turner, *Original Records of Early Nonconformity under Religious Persecution and Indulgence* (London: T. Fisher Unwin, 1911), 1:207–9.

20. Coffey, *Persecution and Toleration*, 173.

21. Wallace describes the impact of this literary output among nonconformist ministers: "Thus there ensued a period of great productivity in the creation of a literature of the spiritual life, and a sharpening of the focus of spirituality upon the drama of the individual soul, in the context of the withdrawn and faithful remnant community." *Spirituality of the Later English Puritans*, xiii–xiv.

Slapton Sands, Devon

nonconformists. Though having a "weak constitution" and "many infirmities," Flavel resumed his
public ministry in a new meeting house built by
the church.[22] There he preached twice every Lord's
Day and Thursday, lectured every Wednesday, and
examined communicants for the Lord's Supper.[23]
According to one account, "When the duty of the
[Lord's Day] was over, he would often complain
of a sore breast, an aching head, and a pained
back; yet he would be early at study again next
Monday."[24] John Galpine describes Flavel's dedica-
tion as follows:

> He was in labors more abundant; he did spend
> himself and was spent in the work of God; as the
> talents committed to him were more and greater
> than many of his brethren, so was his diligence
> in laying them out in his master's service. He
> expected not to be courted to his work by earnest
> importunity, but wheresoever he had any pros-
> pect of doing good by his preaching, I never knew
> him to make excuses or to spare his pains.[25]

Yet Flavel could not continue at this intense pace
indefinitely. On the evening of June 26, 1691, he

---

22. *Life of Flavel*, 1:viii.

23. Flavel was also involved in ministerial training. In 1691, the
Topsham Assembly, a group of Congregationalist and Presbyterian
ministers who met for edification and ministerial training, selected
Flavel as their moderator. Allan Brockett, *Nonconformity in Exeter,
1650–1875* (London: Manchester University Press, 1962), 65.

24. *Life of Flavel*, 1:x.

25. John Galpine, "A Short Life of John Flavel," in *Flavel, the
Quaker and the Crown: John Flavel, Clement Lake, and Religious Liberty
in 17th Century England* (repr., Cambridge, Mass.: Rhwymbooks,
2000), 13.

experienced numbness in his hands. The effects of the stroke quickly spread to the rest of his body. As his family and friends carried him upstairs, he knew death approached but stated "I know that it will be well with me."[26] A few days later, he was laid to rest in the churchyard at St. Savior's. His memorial reads as follows:

Could Grace of Learning from the Grave set free
Flavel thou hadst not seen Mortality
Tho' here thy Dusty Part Death's victim lies
Thou by thy Works thyself dost Eternize,
Which Death nor Rust of time shall overthrow:
Whilst thou dost reign above, these live below.[27]

Not long after his death, Flavel became a well-known name on both sides of the Atlantic. In the 1700s, his writings resonated with the preachers of the Great Awakening. Jonathan Edwards, for example, quoted Flavel extensively in both *Some Thoughts Concerning the Revival* and *Religious Affections*.[28] A woman who was familiar with George Whitefield's sermons stated that the theology of the "New Lights" was not new at all: "It may be new to such as never saw it before; but it is what I saw fifty

---

26. *Life of Flavel*, 1:xv.

27. Ray Freeman, *John Flavel: A Famous Dartmouth Puritan* (Dartmouth, U.K.: Dartmouth History Research Group, 2001), 6.

28. Jonathan Edwards, *The Great Awakening*, in *The Works of Jonathan Edwards*, ed. C. C. Goen (New Haven, Conn.: Yale University Press, 1972), 4:311–12, and John E. Smith, editor's introduction to *Religious Affections*, by Jonathan Edwards, in *The Works of Jonathan Edwards*, ed. John E. Smith (New Haven, Conn.: Yale University Press, 1959), 2:60–62.

years ago, from good Mr. Flavel."[29] His writings also had a tremendous influence on Princeton Seminary's first theology professor, Archibald Alexander (1772–1851), who acknowledged:

> I now began to read Flavel for my own instruction in Christian doctrine. This year, 1788–89, was in many respects the most important of my life. If I had not the beginning of a work of grace, my mind was enlightened by the knowledge of the truth, of which I had lived in total ignorance. I began to love the truth, and to seek after it as for hid treasure. To John Flavel I certainly owe more than to any uninspired author.[30]

Perhaps the most compelling example of the lasting effect of Flavel's writings is Robert Murray M'Cheyne's account of a New England farmer named Luke Short, who had lived in Dartmouth at one time and had been converted through Flavel's sermon on 1 Corinthians 16:22: "If any man love not the Lord Jesus Christ, let him be Anathema Maranatha [accursed]." M'Cheyne explains:

> When he was a hundred years old, he was able to work on his farm, and his mind was not at all impaired. He had lived all this time

---

29. Robert Philip, *The Life and Times of the Reverend George Whitefield* (New York: D. Appleton and Co., 1838), 154. Mark Noll defines the New Lights as follows: "The New England Congregationalists, Baptists, and Separates who favored the revivals of the 1740s and who usually adopted some form of Jonathan Edwards' theology." *America's God: From Jonathan Edwards to Abraham Lincoln* (New York: Oxford University Press, 2002), 566.

30. Charles Hodge, "Memoir of Archibald Alexander," *Biblical Repertory and Princeton Review*, 27, no. 1 (1855): 145–46.

in carelessness and sin; he was a sinner a hundred years old, and ready to die accursed. One day, as he sat in his field, he busied himself in reflecting on his past life. He thought of the days of his youth. His memory fixed on Mr. Flavel's sermon, a considerable part of which he remembered. The earnestness of the minister, the truths spoken, the effect on the people, all came fresh to his mind. He felt that he had not loved the Lord Jesus; he feared the dreadful anathema; he was deeply convicted of sin, was brought to the blood of sprinkling. He lived to his one hundredth and sixteenth year, giving every evidence of being born again.[31]

Theology of Keeping the Heart

How do we account for the spiritual legacy of Flavel's writings? First, he made much of Christ: "No subject can be more necessary to study, or sweet to experience [than Christ]," for, "all goodness is attractive, how powerfully attractive then must Jesus Christ be, who is the ocean of all goodness, from whom all streams of goodness are derived, and into them all empty themselves?"[32] In the words of John Galpine, Flavel was preoccupied with "the glory of God and the good of His church and of the souls of men.... He was well acquainted with the mysteries of the Gospel, and in special with that admirable mystery of

---

31. Robert Murray M'Cheyne, *The Works of the Late Rev. Robert Murray M'Cheyne Complete in Two Volumes* (New York: Robert Carter, 1847), 2:221–22.

32. John Flavel, *The Method of Grace in the Gospel Redemption*, in *The Works of John Flavel* (Edinburgh: Banner of Truth, 1997), 2:6.

man's redemption by Jesus Christ."[33] Flavel preached that the great aim of the gospel is "to open the heart of God to men" and "to set open the heart of man to receive Jesus Christ."[34] Though sinners set their hearts against Christ, He draws them to Himself so that they willingly respond to His rule.[35] Furthermore, Flavel stressed communion with God through Christ: "True religion seats itself in the inward man, and acts effectually upon the vital power, killing sin in the heart, and engaging the heart for God."[36] This led Flavel to address "experimental subjects as communion with God, prayer, and the life of faith."[37] Finally, Flavel wrote from the vantage point of Christian experience. He "spoke from his own heart to others. He preached what he felt, what he had handled, what he had seen and tasted of the word of life, and they felt it also."[38]

---

33. Galpine, *Short Life of John Flavel*, 11–12. As Iain Murray notes, Flavel's writings were "thoroughly and consistently evangelical." "John Flavel," *The Banner of Truth* 60 (1968): 5.

34. John Flavel, *England's Duty under the Present Gospel Liberty: Eleven Sermons on Revelation 3:20*, in *The Works of John Flavel* (Edinburgh: Banner of Truth, 1997), 4:194.

35. Flavel, *England's Duty*, 4:196–97.

36. John Flavel, *The Touchstone of Sincerity: or, The Signs of Grace, and Symptoms of Hypocrisy. Opened in a Treatise upon Revelation 3:17, 18,* in *The Works of John Flavel* (Edinburgh: Banner of Truth, 1997), 5:518. *Signs of Grace* is the follow-up volume to *A Saint Indeed / Keeping the Heart*. Though not as popular as the first volume, it was originally printed in 1679 (London) and reprinted in 1684 (Edinburgh), 1698 (London), and 1707 (Glasgow). In America, it was republished in 1731 (Boston), 1795 (Amherst, N.H.), 1809 (New Haven, Conn.), 1814, and 1818 (Boston).

37. Murray, "John Flavel," 7.

38. *Life of Flavel*, 1:xii. The author's words echo 1 John 1:1.

The reason, therefore, behind Flavel's popularity was his skill as a physician of the heart. He affirmed that, in the covenant of grace, there is "an intimate conjunction of believers to Christ, by the imparting of his Spirit to them, whereby they are enabled to believe and live in him."[39] We might not understand "how the Spirit of God first entered into, and quickened our souls," but we "experimentally feel, and sensibly discern" the effects of His power.[40] These effects are discerned through God's appointed means of grace, such as listening and meditation on Scripture, prayer, the Lord's Supper, and Christian fellowship. As Flavel makes clear, God appointed "so many ordinances and duties of religion, on purpose to maintain daily communion between Christ and his people."[41] Consequently, for Flavel, the goal of keeping the heart is to foster "actual fellowship or communion...with Christ in holy duties, wherein Christians let forth their hearts to God by desires, and God lets forth his comforts and refreshments into their hearts."[42] Stephen Yuille describes this emphasis as follows:

> Keeping watch over the soul is foundational to other spiritual duties, because their effectiveness depends in large part upon the removal of those encumbrances that dampen the affections.

---

39. Flavel, *Method of Grace*, in *Works*, 2:37. Also see *An Exposition of the (Westminster) Assembly's Shorter Catechism, with Practical Inferences from Each Question (as Carried on at Dartmouth in 1688)*, in *The Works of John Flavel* (Edinburgh: Banner of Truth, 1997), 6:174–77.

40. Flavel, *Method of Grace*, 2:351.

41. Flavel, *England's Duty*, 4:247.

42. Flavel, *Method of Grace*, 2:144.

Unconfessed sin, unchecked pride, and undisciplined thoughts tend to render the soul insensible to any "influences" that God sets forth in duties. Our first responsibility, therefore, is to remove all hindrances to communion.[43]

Yet, as a seasoned pastor, Flavel had observed that the heart was deceitful above all else (Jer. 17:9), and so "many professors are only acquainted with the external [duties] of religion; and all their duties are no more but a compliance of the outward man with the commands of God."[44] For these individuals it is "not their business to have fellowship with God in duties, get their lusts mortified, their hearts tried, their souls conformed to the image of God in holiness."[45] True believers, on the other hand, are led by the Spirit to discern their hearts as they appropriate the means of grace, especially when they join their hearts together with the Word in self-examination.[46] Flavel explains how the Spirit works with the Word to help believers discern the evidences of grace in their hearts:

It is very observable, that the works of grace wrought by the Spirit in the hearts of believers,

---

43. J. Stephen Yuille, *The Inner Sanctum of Puritan Piety: John Flavel's Doctrine of Mystical Union with Christ* (Grand Rapids: Reformation Heritage Books, 2007), 96. In chapter 10, Yuille expands on Flavel's view of practicing union with Christ through listening and meditating on Scripture, praying, and partaking of the Lord's Supper.

44. Flavel, *Signs of Grace*, 5:518. Flavel's brother Phineas preached sermons on Jeremiah 17:9 and published them as *The Grand Evil Discovered: or, The Deceitful Heart Tried and Cast Being the Substance of Some Sermons Preached from Jeremiah 17:9* (London, 1676).

45. Flavel, *Signs of Grace*, 5:521.

46. See how Flavel examined his heart in selection 13.

are represented to us in scripture, as a transcript, or copy of the written word, Jer. xxxi. 33. "I will write my law in their hearts." Now, as a true copy answers the original, word for word, letter for letter, point for point; so do the works of the Spirit in our souls harmonize with the dictates of the Spirit in the scriptures.[47]

For Flavel, "keeping the heart" is a lifetime work: "You find in the Word, a world of work cut out for Christians; there is hearing-work, praying-work, reading, meditating, and self-examining work; it puts him also upon a constant watch over all the corruptions of his heart. Oh, what a world of work hath a Christian about him?"[48] For this reason, he affirms "that the keeping and the right managing of the heart in every condition, is the great business of a Christian's life."[49]

In the remainder of this book, I have selected passages from Flavel's writings where this "great business" is best represented. My desire is that, as you read, you will carry out the encouragement that Flavel gave his people centuries ago: "Above all other studies in the world, study your own hearts."[50]

47. Flavel, *Method of Grace*, 2:345.

48. Flavel, *Husbandry Spiritualized*, 5:28.

49. Flavel, *A Saint Indeed: or, The Great Work of a Christian, Opened and Pressed. From Prov. 4:23*, in *The Works of John Flavel* (Edinburgh: Banner of Truth, 1997), 5:425.

50. Flavel, *Saint Indeed*, 5:421.

SECTION ONE

Christ Rules the Heart

A Chart of English Ships by Devonshire
(National Maritime Museum, Greenwich, England)

Flavel ministered for some time in the naval city
of Dartmouth. Several of his books were written
specifically to minister to sailors.

1

To Win and Gain
the Hearts of Sinners

Behold, I stand at the door, and knock:
if any man hear my voice, and open the door,
I will come in to him, and sup with him,
and he with me. —Revelation 3:20

This text is Christ's wooing voice, full of heavenly rhetoric to win and gain the hearts of sinners to Himself, wherein we have these two general parts....

First, *Christ's suit for a sinner's heart*, wherein we have, first, the solemn preface, ushering it in—"behold"—and, second, the suit itself. The preface is exceedingly solemn, for beside the common use of this word *behold* in other places to excite attention or exaggerate and put weight into an affirmation, it stands here, as a judicious expositor[1] notes, as a term of notification, or public record, wherein Christ takes witness of the most gracious offer He was now about to make to their souls, and will have it stand...as a testimony for or against their souls to all eternity, to cut off all excuses and pretences for time to come.

From *England's Duty,* in *Works*, 4:17–20.

1. The expositor Flavel referenced was the Scottish professor of divinity at Glasgow University, James Durham, and his book, *A Commentarie upon the Book of the Revelation* (London, 1658).

Second, the suit itself, wherein we have the following:

1. The suitor Christ Himself: "I stand." I that have a right of sovereignty over you; I that have shed My invaluable blood to purchase you and might justly condemn you upon the first denial or demur, "Behold I stand." This is the Suitor.

2. His posture and action: "I stand at the door and knock." The word is in the [past] tense ("I have stood"), but being here joined with another verb of the present tense, it is fitly translated "I stand," yet so as that it notes a continued action. "I have stood and do still stand with unwearied patience; I once stood personally and bodily among you in the days of My flesh, and I still stand spiritually and representatively in my ambassadors at the door, that is, the mind and conscience, the faculties and powers which are intro-ductive into the whole soul."

The word *door* is here improperly put to signify those introductive faculties of the soul that are of a like use to it, as the door is to the house. This is the Redeemer's posture—His action is knocking, that is, His powerful efforts and gracious attempts to open the heart to give Him admission. The word *knock* signifies a strong and powerful knock; He stands patiently and knocks powerfully by the Word outwardly, by the convictions, motions, impulses, strivings, and instigations of His Spirit inwardly.

3. The design and end of the suit: it is for opening, that is, consenting, receiving, embracing, and hearty accepting of Him by faith. In Acts 16:14 the Lord

opened the heart of Lydia, that is, persuaded her soul to believe, implying that the heart by nature is strongly barred and locked up against Christ, and nothing but power from Him can open it.

Second, the powerful arguments and motives Christ used to obtain His suit and get a grant from the sinner's heart, and they are drawn from two inestimable benefits accruing to the opening or believing soul.

4. Union—"I will come in to him," that is, I will unite Myself with the opening, believing soul. He shall be mystically one with Me, and I with him.

5. Communion—"I will...sup with him, and he with me"; that is, I will feast the believing soul with the [delicacies] of heaven. Such comforts, such joys, such pleasures as none in the world but believers are capable of.

And to set home all, Christ proposed these special benefits to all sorts of sinners great and small, old and young ("if any man hear my voice, and open the door"), that so no soul might be discouraged from believing by the greatness or multitude of his sins, but the vilest of sinners may see free grace triumphing over all their unworthiness upon their consent to take Christ according to the gracious offers of the gospel.

2

Shutting up the Heart against Christ

That all hearts are naturally shut and made fast against Christ is a sad but certain truth; we read in John 1:11–12: "He came unto his own, and his own received him not." Christ found the doors of men's hearts generally shut against Him, except for only a few whose hearts were opened by the almighty power of God in the way of faith (v. 12); these indeed received Him, but all the rest excluded and denied entrance to the Son of God.

Now there is a twofold shutting up of the heart against Jesus Christ. First, a natural one: every soul comes into this world shut up and fast closed against the Lord Jesus. The very will of man that is the freest and most arbitrary faculty comes into the world barred and bolted against Christ: "The carnal mind is enmity against God: for it is not subject to the law of God, neither indeed can be" (Rom. 8:7). "It is God which worketh in you both to will and to do of his own good pleasure" (Phil. 2:13). This is a dismal effect of the fall: who feels not strong [aversions], violent rebellions, and obstinate resistances in his own

From *England's Duty*, in *Works*, 4:42–43.

heart when moving toward Christ in the first weak and trembling acts of faith?

Second, here is a judicial shutting up of the heart against Christ. This is a sore and tremendous stroke of God, punishing former rebellions: "Israel would [have] none of me, so I gave them up unto their own hearts' lusts" (Ps. 81:11–12). This looks like a prelude of damnation, a very near preparation to ruin. "Israel would have none of me"—there's the natural shutting up of the heart. "So I gave them up"—there's the judicial shutting up of the heart; they would not hear, they shall not hear. Oh fearful judgment! Thus the Lord gave up the heathens (Rom. 1:26). They had abused their natural light, and now their minds are judicially darkened, given up to a sottish[1] and injudicious mind, not able to distinguish duty from sin, safety from danger; a mind that should elect the worst things, and reprobate the best.... These two closures of the hearts are not always found together, in the same subject, and blessed be God they are not. Christ meets with many a repulse and endures with much patience the gain-sayings of sinners before He pronounces that dreadful sentence upon them: "Go, and tell this people, Hear ye indeed, but understand not; and see ye indeed, but perceive not: Make the heart of this people [dull]" (Isa. 6:9–10).[2]

---

1. *sottish*: drunken

3

The Great Design
and Aim of the Gospel

The powerful voice of Christ is the key that opens the door of the soul to receive Him. The opening of the heart to receive Christ is the main design aimed at in all the external and internal administrations of the gospel and Spirit.

The gospel has two great designs and intentions. One is to open the heart of God to men and to show them the everlasting counsels of grace and peace that were hid in God from ages and generations past, that all men may now see that God had been designing and contriving for their happiness in Christ before the world was: "To make all men see what is the fellowship of the mystery, which from the beginning of the world hath been hid in God, who created all things by Jesus Christ, to the intent that now unto the principalities and powers in heavenly places might be known by the church the manifold wisdom of God" (Eph. 3:9).

The next intention and aim of the gospel is to set open the heart of man to receive Jesus Christ, without which all the glorious discoveries of the eternal counsels and gracious contrivances of God

From *England's Duty*, in *Works*, 4:193–94.

for and about us would signify nothing to our real advantage. Christ standing, knocking, and speaking by His Spirit (of which we have before treated) receive their success and attain their end when the heart opens itself by faith to receive Him, and not till then. Hence, note that the opening of the heart to receive Christ by faith is the great design and aim of the gospel.

Great persons have great designs. This is the glorious project of the great God, and every person in the Godhead is engaged and concerned in it. (1) The Father has His hand in this work, and such a hand as without it no heart could ever open or move in the least towards Christ: "No man can come unto me [Christ says] except the Father which hath sent me draw him" (John 6:44). None but He that raised up Christ from the dead can raise up a dead heart unto saving faith in Him. (2) The Son's hand is in this work; He is not only the object but the author of our faith: "We know that the Son of God is come, and hath given us an understanding, that we may know him that is true, and we are in him that is true, even in his Son Jesus Christ. This is the true God, and eternal life" (1 John 5:20). (3) And then for the Spirit, He comes from heaven designedly and expressly to convince sinners of their need of Christ and beget faith in them, so that this appears to be the great design of heaven (John 16:9).

4

A Throne in the Hearts of Men

We will open the way and manner in which Christ obtains a throne in the hearts of men, and that is by conquest. For though the souls of the elect are His by donation and right of redemption, the Father gave them to Him, and He died for them—yet Satan had the first possession; and so…Christ must fight His way into the soul, though He have right to enter as into His dearly purchased possession. And so He does, for when the time of recovering them is come, He sends forth His armies to subdue them. As it is in Psalm 110:3: "Thy people shall be willing in the day of thy power."… The Lord Jesus sent forth His armies of prophets, apostles, evangelists, pastors, and teachers, under the conduct of His Spirit, armed with that two-edged sword, the Word of God, which is sharp and powerful (Heb. 4:12). But that is not all: He causes armies of convictions and spiritual troubles to begird and straiten them on every side, so that they know not what to do. These convictions, like a shower of arrows, strike point blank into their consciences. "When they heard this, they were pricked in their heart, and said unto Peter and to the rest of

From *Fountain of Life*, in *Works*, 1:200–203.

the apostles, Men and brethren, what shall we do?"
(Acts 2:37). Christ's arrows are sharp in the hearts of
His enemies....

Now all their weak pleas and defenses, from the
general mercy of God, the examples of others, etc.,
prove but as paper walls to them. These shake their
hearts, even to the foundation, and overturn every
high thought there that exalts itself against the Lord.
This day in which Christ sits down before the soul
and summons it by such messengers as these is a
day of distress within; yea, such a day of trouble
that none is like it.... Sometimes there is no hope—
"Christ will slay me if I go forth to Him"—and
then it trembles. But then, "Whoever found Him so
that tried Him? Other souls have yielded and found
mercy beyond all their expectation. Oh but I have
been a desperate enemy against Him."

A thousand such debates there are, till at last,
the soul considering, if it abide in rebellion, it must
perish; if it go forth to Christ, it can but perish; and
being somewhat encouraged by the messages of
grace sent into the soul at this time, such as Hebrews
7:25 ("Wherefore he is able also to save them to the
uttermost that come unto God by him"); and John
6:37 ("Him that cometh to me I will in no wise cast
out"); and Matthew 11:28 ("Come unto me, all ye
that labour and are heavy laden, and I will give you
rest"). It is, at last, resolved to open to Christ and says,
"Lift up your heads, O ye gates; and be ye lift up, ye
everlasting doors; and the King of glory shall come
in" [Psalm 24:7]. Now the will spontaneously opens

to Christ. That Fort Royal[1] submits and yields....
Thus it comes in to Christ by free and hearty submission, desiring nothing more than to come under the
government of Christ for the time to come.

---

1. *Fort Royal*: An English Civil War fort constructed by the
Royalists in 1651 on a small hill southeast of Worcester. During the
last battle of the war, the Parliamentarians stormed and captured
Fort Royal and ultimately were victorious.

5

— ⊳ ◦(◦)◦ ◦ —

Jesus Christ Most
Heartily Approved

Our receiving Christ necessarily implies our hearty approbation,[1] liking, and estimation, yes, the acquiescence of our very souls in Jesus Christ, as the most excellent, suitable, and complete remedy for all our wants, sins, and dangers that ever could be prepared by the wisdom and love of God for them. We must receive Him with such a frame of heart as rests upon Him, trusts and relies upon Him, if ever we receive Him aright.... And therefore as Christ is most highly esteemed and heartily approved as the only remedy for our souls, so the sovereign grace and wisdom of God are admired, and the way and method He has taken to save poor lost souls by Jesus Christ most heartily approved as the most apt and excellent method, both for His glory and our good, that ever could be taken....

There are two things in Christ that must gain the greatest approbation in the soul of a poor, convinced sinner and bring it to rest upon Jesus Christ.

First, that it can find nothing in Christ that is distasteful or unsuitable to it, as it doth experimentally

---

From *Method of Grace,* in *Works*, 2:106–9.

1. *approbation*: an act of approving formally or officially

find in the best creatures. In Him is no weakness but a fullness of all saving abilities: "able to save to the uttermost" [Heb. 7:25]; no pride causing Him to scorn and condemn the most wretched soul that comes to Him; no inconsistency or levity to cause Him to cast off the soul whom He has once received; no passion,[2] but a lamb for meekness and patience; there is not a spot to be found in Him, but "he is altogether lovely" (Song 5:16).

Second, as the believer can find nothing in Christ that is distasteful, so he finds nothing wanting in Christ that is necessary or desirable. Such is the fullness of wisdom, righteousness, sanctification, and redemption that is in Christ, that nothing is left to desire but the full enjoyment of Him. "O," says the soul, "How completely happy shall I be, if I can but win Christ! I would not envy the nobles of the earth, were I but in Christ. I am hungry and thirsty, and Christ is meat indeed and drink indeed; this is the best thing in all the world for me, because it is so necessary and so suitable to the needs of a soul ready to perish. I am law condemned and a self-condemned sinner, trembling for fear of execution of the curse upon me every moment; in Christ is complete righteousness to justify my soul. O there is nothing better for me than Christ. I see myself plunged both in nature and practice into the odious pollutions of sin, and in Christ is a fountain opened for sin and for uncleanness. His blood is a fountain of merit, His spirit a fountain of holiness and purity. None but Christ, none but Christ. O the manifold

---

2. *passion*: uncontrolled emotions

wisdom and unsearchable love of God to prepare and furnish such a Christ, so fully answering all the needs, all the distresses, all the fears and burdens of a poor sinner!"

6

---===--- ◆ ---===---

Consolations for an
Opened Heart

Has God indeed opened any of your hearts and made you sincerely willing to receive Christ? Then there are ten sweet consolations, like so many boxes of precious ointment, to be poured forth in the close of this discourse upon every such soul.

1. The first is this: the opening of any man's heart to receive Christ is a clear, solid Scripture evidence of the Lord's eternal love to and setting apart that man for Himself from all eternity.... A more clear and certain evidence of your election cannot be given in this world; look again into Romans 8:30: "Moreover whom he did predestinate, them he also called: and whom he called, them he also justified: and whom he justified, them he also glorified."

2. The opening of the heart to receive Christ is the peculiar effect of the divine and almighty power of God; the arm of an angel is too weak to break those strong bars before mentioned.[1] Therefore the exceeding greatness of His power is applied unto this work of

---

From *England's Duty*, in *Works*, 4:58–63.

1. The "strong bars" around sinners' hearts that keep Christ out of the heart include ignorance, unbelief, pride, sinful habits, presumption of grace, and prejudice against holiness.

believing: "And what is the exceeding greatness of his power to us-ward who believe, according to the working of his mighty power, which he wrought in Christ, when he raised him from the dead" (Eph. 1:19–20). Here is power, the power of God, the greatness of His power, the exceeding greatness of His power, the very same power that was wrought in Christ when He raised Him from the dead; and all this no more than needs to make the heart of man open by faith to receive Christ. The only key that fits the cross wards[2] of man's will and effectually opens his heart is in the hand of Christ: "He that hath the key of David, he that openeth, and no man shutteth" (Rev. 3:7).

3. The opening of your heart to Christ is not only an effect of almighty power, but such an effect of it, that without it, all Christ had done and suffered would have been of no avail to your salvation. Neither the eternal decrees of God nor the meritorious sufferings of Christ are effectual to any man's salvation, until this work of the Spirit is wrought upon his heart.

4. In this work of the opening of the heart by faith, the great design and main intention of the gospel is also answered and accomplished.... Ministers are sent "to open [your] eyes, and to turn [you] from darkness to light, and from the power of Satan to God" (Acts 26:18).

5. And then fifthly, that day wherein your heart is savingly opened to receive Christ, that very day is salvation come to your soul. When Zaccheus's heart

---

2. *cross wards*: a place of protection

was opened to Christ, He tells him, "This day is salvation come to this house" (Luke 19:9).

6. The opening of a sinner's heart to Christ makes joy in heaven, a triumph in the city of our God above: "I say unto you, that likewise joy shall be in heaven over one sinner that repenteth, more than over ninety and nine just persons, which need no repentance" (Luke 15:7).... Beloved, when the gospel is effectually brought home by the Spirit to the heart of a sinner and wounds him for sin, sends him home crying, oh sick, sick—sick for sin, and sick for Christ—the news thereof is presently in heaven and sets the whole city of God rejoicing. Christ never rejoiced over you before—you have wounded Him and grieved Him a thousand times, but He never rejoiced in you till now—and that which gives joy to Christ may well be matter of joy to you.

7. And then seventhly, that day your heart is unlocked, unbarred, and savingly opened by faith, that very day an intimate, spiritual, and everlasting union is made between Christ and your soul; from that day Christ is yours, and you are His. Christ is a great and glorious person, but however great and glorious He be, the small and feeble arms of your faith may surround and embrace Him, and you may say with the church, "My beloved is mine, and I am his" [Song 2:16]; for mark what He says in the text [Rev. 3:20]: "If any man open to Me, I will come in to him. That soul shall be My habitation. There will I dwell forever." So, then, Christ may dwell in your hearts by faith. What soul feels not itself advanced by this union with the Son of God?

8. And then in the eighth place, the opening of your heart to Christ brings you not only into union with His person, but into a state of sweet, soul-enriching communion with Him. So he speaks in the text [Rev. 3:20]: "If any man open the door, I will sup with him and he with Me."... Now you may say, "Truly my fellowship is with the Father and with His Son, Jesus Christ" (1 John 1:3).

9. The opening of a man's soul to Christ by faith is a special and peculiar mercy that falls to the share but of a very few.... The sound of the gospel is gone forth into the world; "many are called, but few are chosen" [Matt. 22:14].

10. And then lastly, in the same day your heart opens by faith to Christ, all the treasures of Christ are unlocked and opened to you. In the same hour God turns the key of regeneration to open your soul, the key of free grace is also turned to open unto you the unsearchable riches of Christ. Then the righteousness of Christ becomes yours to justify you, the wisdom of Christ to guide you, the holiness of Christ to sanctify you; in a word, He is that day, made of God unto you, "wisdom, and righteousness, and sanctification, and redemption" (1 Cor. 1:30). "All is yours, for you are Christ's, and Christ is God's" (1 Cor. 3.23).

SECTION TWO

Keeping the Heart

University College, Oxford

Flavel excelled in his studies at Oxford, graduating in 1650. Evidencing his practical aim in gaining knowledge, Flavel said that "all our reading, studying, and preaching is but trifling hypocrisy till…felt in some degree upon our own hearts."

7

➤►◄(●)►◄◄

Above All Other Studies

Of the relation I have to you above all the people in the world: I look upon my gifts as yours, my time as yours, and all the talents I am entrusted with as yours.... I was willing to leave this [book] with you as a legacy, as a testimony of sincere love for and care over you. This may counsel and direct you when I cannot. I may be rendered useless to you by a civil or natural death, but this will outlive me, and oh that it may serve your souls when I am silent in the dust!

I have only these three requests of you....

(1) Above all other studies in the world, study your own hearts: waste not a minute more of your precious time about frivolous and sapless controversies.... My dear flock, I have, according to the grace given me, labored in the course of my ministry among you to feed you with the heart-strengthening bread of practical doctrine, and I assure you, it is far better you should have the sweet and saving impressions of gospel truths, feelingly and powerfully conveyed to your hearts, than only to understand them by a bare ratiocination[1] or a dry, syllogistical inference. Leave trifling studies to those who have

---

From *A Saint Indeed*, in *Works*, 5:420–24.

1. *ratiocination*: methodical or logical reasoning

time lying on their hands and do not know how to employ it. Remember you are at the door of eternity and have other work to do; those hours you spend upon heart-work in your closets are the golden spots of all your time and will have the sweetest influence into your last hour.... Heart-work is weighty and difficult work; an error there may cost you your souls.... O, then, study your hearts.

(2) My next request is that you will carefully look to your conversations[2] and be accurate in all your ways; hold forth the word of life.... Oh then be precise and accurate in all manner of conversation; keep up the power of godliness in your closets and families, and then you will not let it fall in your more public employments and converses in the world. I have often told you that it is the honor of the gospel, that it makes the best parents and children, the best masters and servants, the best husbands and wives in the world.

(3) My third and last request is that you pray for me.... I have often prayed for you.... Yea, friends, your own interest may persuade to it. What mercies you obtain for me [through prayer], redound to your own advantage. If God preserve me, it is for your use and service: the more gifts and graces a minister has, the better for them that shall wait on his ministry. The more God give in to me, the more I shall be able to give out to you.

Your loving and faithful pastor,
John Flavel

From my study at Ley, in Slapton, October 7, 1667

---

2. *conversations*: lives

8

—◆◆◆—

The Great Business

*Keep thy heart with all diligence; for out of it
are the issues of life.* —Proverbs 4:23

The heart of man is his worst part before it is regenerated, and the best afterwards. It is the seat of principles and fountain of actions. The eye of God is, and the eye of the Christian ought to be, principally fixed upon it.

The greatest difficulty in conversion is to win the heart to God, and the greatest difficulty after conversion is to keep the heart with God. Here lies the very pinch and stress of religion; here's that thing that makes the way to life a narrow way, and the gate of heaven a strait gate....

"Heart" is not here [in Proverbs 4:23] taken properly for that noble part of the body...but by "heart" in a metaphor, the Scripture sometimes understands some particular noble faculty of the soul. It is put for the understanding part (Rom 1:21). It is put for the memory (Ps. 119:11). It is put for the conscience, which has in it both the light of the understanding and the recognitions of the memory (1 John 3:10). But here we are to take it more generally for the whole soul, or inner man. For look what the heart

From *A Saint Indeed*, in *Works*, 5:423–25.

is to the body, that the soul is to the man; and what health is to the heart, that holiness is to the soul….

And by "keeping the heart," understand the diligent and constant use and improvement of all holy means and duties to preserve the soul from sin and maintain its sweet and free communion with God…. And whereas the expression ["keep the heart"] seems to put it upon us as our work, yet it does not imply a sufficiency or ability in us to do it…. We may as well be our own saviors as our own keepers, and yet Solomon speaks properly enough when he says, *"Keep the heart,"* because the duty is ours, though the power be God's. A natural man has no power, a gracious man has some, though not sufficient, and the power that he has depends upon the exciting and assisting strength of Christ (John 15:5)….

How important a duty is that which is contained in the following proposition? *That the keeping and the right managing of the heart in every condition is the great business of a Christian's life.*

9

The Pained Place

Well, then, to keep the heart is carefully to preserve it from sin, which disorders it, and maintain that spiritual and gracious frame that fits it for a life of communion with God. And this includes these six acts in it.

1. First, frequent observation of the frame of the heart, turning in and examining how the case stands with it, this is one part of the work. Carnal and formal persons take no heed to this; they cannot be brought to confer with their own hearts. There are some men and women who have lived forty or fifty years in the world and have scarce had one hour's discourse with their own hearts all that while; it is a hard thing to bring a man and himself together upon such an account, but saints know those soliloquies and self-conferences to be of excellent use and advantage.... The heart can never be kept until its case is examined and understood.

2. It includes deep humiliations for heart-evils and disorders; thus Hezekiah humbled himself for the pride of his heart (2 Chron. 32:26). Thus the people were ordered to spread forth their hands to God in prayer, in a sense of the plague of their own hearts

From *A Saint Indeed*, in *Works*, 5:426–28.

(1 Kings 8:38). Upon this account many an upright heart has been laid low before God: O what a heart have I? They have in their confessions pointed at the heart, the pained place. Lord, here is the wound; here is the plague-sore. It is with the heart well kept as it is with the eye, which is a fit emblem of it. If a small particle of dust gets into the eye, it will never stop twinkling and watering until it has wept it out. So the upright heart cannot be at rest until it has wept out its troubles and poured out its complaints before the Lord.

3. It includes earnest supplications and instant prayer for heart-purifying and rectifying grace when sin has defiled and disordered (Pss. 119:12; 86:11). Saints have always many such petitions waiting before the throne of grace; this is the thing they most plead with God. When they are praying for outward mercies, happily their spirits may be more remiss, but when it comes to the heart-case, then they intend their spirits to the upmost, fill their mouths with arguments, weep, and make supplications. Oh, for a better heart! Oh for a heart to love God more! To hate sin more, to walk more evenly with God. Lord, deny not to me such a heart, whatever Thou deny me. Give me a heart to fear Thee, love, and delight in Thee....

4. [Keeping the heart also] includes imposing the strong engagements and bonds upon us to walk more accurately with God and avoid the occasions whereby the heart may be induced to sin. Well composed, advised, and deliberate vows are in some cases of excellent use to guard the heart, against

some special sin, as in Job 31:1: "I made a covenant with my eyes." By this means, holy ones have over-awed their souls and preserved themselves from defilement by some special heart-corruptions.

5. It includes a constant holy jealousy over our own hearts. Quick-sighted self-jealousy is an excellent preservative from sin. He that will keep his heart must have the eyes of his soul awake and open upon all the disorderly and tumultuous stirrings of his affections. If the affections break loose and the passions be stirred, the soul must discover and suppress them before they get to a height: O my soul, do you do well in this? My tumultuous thoughts and passions: Where is your commission?

Happy is the man that thus fears always (Prov. 28:14). By this fear of the Lord it is that men depart from evil, shake off security, and preserve themselves from iniquity. He that will keep his heart must feed with fear, rejoice with fear, and pass the whole time of his sojourning here in fear, and all little enough to keep the heart from sin.

6. And lastly, to add no more, it includes the realizing of God's presence with us and setting the Lord always before us. Thus the people of God have found a singular means to keep their hearts upright and awe them from sin. When the eye of our faith is fixed upon the eye of God's omniscience, we dare not let out our thoughts and affections to vanity. Holy Job dared not suffer his heart to an impure vain thought, and what was it that moved him to so great a circumspection? Why, he tells you in Job 31:4: "Doth not he see my ways, and count all my

steps?" "Walk before me," says God to Abraham, "and be thou perfect" (Gen. 17:1). Even as parents set their children in the congregation before them, knowing that otherwise they will be toying and playing, so would the heart of the best man, too, were it not for the eye of God.

10

The Most Difficult, Constant, and Important Work

This is the work, and of all works in religion it is the most difficult, constant, and important work.

1. It's the hardest work; heart work is hard work indeed. To shuffle over religious duties with a loose and heedless spirit will cost no great pains, but to set yourself before the Lord and tie up the loose and vain thoughts to a constant and serious attendance upon Him, this will cost you something. To attain a facility and dexterity of language in prayer and put your meaning into apt and decent expressions is easy, but to get your heart broken for sin while you are confessing it; melted with free grace while you are blessing God for it; to be really ashamed and humbled through the apprehensions of God's infinite holiness and to keep your heart in this frame, not only in, but after duty will surely cost you some groans and travailing pains of the soul. To repress the outward acts of sin and compose the external part of your life in a laudable and comely manner is no great matter; even carnal persons by the force of common principles can do this. But to kill the root of corruption within, to set and keep up a holy government

From *A Saint Indeed*, in *Works*, 5:428–29.

over your thoughts, to have all things lie straight and orderly in the heart, this is not easy.

2. It's a constant work; the keeping of the heart is such a work as is never done till life is done. This labor and our life end together.... There is no time or condition in the life of a Christian that will suffer an intermission of this work.... You know it cost David and Peter many a sad day and night for intermitting the watch over their own hearts but a few minutes (2 Sam. 11; Matt. 26:30–35, 69–75).

3. It's the most important business of a Christian life. Without this we are but formalists in religion: all our professions, gifts, and duties signify nothing.... God rejects all duties (however glorious in other respects) offered Him without a heart, he that performs duty without a heart, namely, heedlessly, is no more accepted with God, than he that performs it with a double heart, that is, hypocritically (Isa. 66:3).

11

A Sincere Christian
in His Closet

[John Flavel] was not only a zealous preacher in the pulpit, but a sincere Christian in his closet, frequent in self-examination as well as in pressing it upon others—being afraid, lest while he preached to others he himself should be a castaway. To prove this, I shall transcribe what follows from his own diary:

> To make sure of eternal life is the great business which the sons of death have to do in this world. Whether a man consider the immortality of his own soul, the ineffable joys and glory of heaven, the extreme and endless torments of hell, the inconceivable sweetness of peace of conscience, or the misery of being subject to the terrors thereof, all these put a necessity, a solemnity, a glory upon this work [of self-examination]. But, oh, the difficulties and dangers attending it! How many and how great are these? What judgment, faithfulness, resolution, and watchfulness does it require? Such is the deceitfulness, darkness, and inconstancy of our hearts, and such the malice, policy, and diligence of Satan to manage and improve it, that he who attempts this work had need both to

watch his seasons for it and frequently look up to God for His guidance and illumination and to spend many sad and serious thoughts before he adventure upon a determination and conclusion of the state of his soul.

To the end therefore that this most important work may not miscarry in my hands, I have collected, with all the care I can, the best and soundest characters I can find in the writings of our modern divines,[1] taken out of the Scripture, and by their labors illustrated and prepared for use, that I might make a right application of them.

I have earnestly sought the Lord for the assistance of His Spirit, which can only manifest my own heart unto me and show me the true state thereof, which is that thing my soul does most earnestly desire to know; and I hope the Lord will answer my desire therein, according to His promises (Luke 11:13; John 14:26).

I have endeavored to cast out and lay aside self-love, lest my heart being prepossessed therewith, my judgment should be perverted and become partial on passing sentence on my estate. I have, in some measure, brought my heart to be willing to judge and condemn

---

1. When setting down a list of guidelines for self-examination similar to those in his diary, Flavel quoted from other Puritans, "modern divines" such as William Gurnall's *The Christian in Complete Armor*; Obadiah Sedgwick's *The Anatomy of Secret Sins*; Cuthbert Sydenham's *The Greatness of the Mystery of Godliness Together with Hypocrisy Discovered in Its Nature and Workings*. See Flavel's Antipharmacum Saluberrimum: *or, A Serious and Seasonable Caveat to All the Saints in This Hour of Temptation,* in *The Works of John Flavel* (London: Banner of Truth, 1968), 4:552–57.

myself for a hypocrite, if such I shall be found on trial, as to approve myself for sincere and upright. Yea, I would have it so far from being grievous to me so to do, that if I have been all this while mistaken and deceived, I shall rejoice and bless the Lord with my soul, that now at last it may be discovered to me and I may be set right, though I lay the foundation new again. This I have labored to bring my heart to, knowing that thousands have dashed and split to pieces upon this rock; and indeed he that will own the person of a judge must put off the person of a friend.

It has been my endeavor to keep upon my heart a deep sense of that great judgment day throughout this work, as knowing by experience what a potent influence this has on the conscience, to make it deliberate, serious, and faithful in its work. And therefore I have demanded of my own conscience, before the resolutions of each question, O my conscience, deal faithfully with me in this particular, and say no more to me than you will own and stand to in the great day, when the counsels of all hearts shall be made manifest.

Having seriously weighed each mark and considered wherein the weight and substance of it lies, I have gone to the Lord in prayer for His assistance, ere I have drawn up the answer of my conscience; and as my heart has been persuaded therein, so have I determined and resolved: what has been clear to my experience, I have so set down, and what has been dubious, I have here left it so.

I have made choice of the fittest seasons I had for this work and set to it when I have found my heart in the most quiet and serious frame. For as he that would see his face in a glass must be fixed, not in motion or in water, must make no commotion in it, so it is in this case.

To the end I may be successful in this work, I have labored all along carefully to distinguish between such sins as are grounds of doubting, and such as are only grounds of humiliation, knowing that not every evil is a ground of doubting, though all, even the smallest infirmities, administer matter of humiliation; and thus I have desired to enterprise this great business. O Lord, assist Thy servant, that he may not mistake herein; but, if his conscience does now condemn him, he may lay a better foundation while he has time; and if it shall now acquit him, he may also have boldness in the day of judgment.

These things being previously dispatched, he tried himself by the Scripture marks of sincerity and regeneration. By this means he attained to a well-grounded assurance, the ravishing comforts of which were many times shed abroad in his soul. This made him a powerful and successful preacher, as one who spoke from his own heart to those of others. He preached what he felt, what he had handled, what he had seen and tasted of the word of life, and [his hearers] felt it also.

12

The Best Schoolmaster

All that I beg for is but this, that you would step aside a little oftener to talk with God and your own heart, that you would not suffer every trifle to divert you, that you would keep a more true and faithful account of your thoughts and affections, that you would but seriously demand of your own heart, at least every evening, *O my heart, where have you been today*? I have yet more motives to offer you. And the first is this.

The studying, observing, and diligent keeping of your own hearts will marvelously keep your understanding in the deep mysteries of religion. An honest, well-experienced heart is a singular help to a weak head; such a heart will serve you instead of a commentary upon a great part of the Scriptures; by this means you shall far better understand the things of God than the learned rabbis and profound doctors (if graceless and inexperienced) ever did. You shall not only have a clearer but a more sweet perception and gust of them. A man may discourse orthodoxly and profoundly of the nature and effects of faith, the troubles and comforts of conscience, the sweetness of communion with God, that never felt the efficacy and sweet impressions of these things upon his own spirit. But oh how dark and dry are those notions,

From *A Saint Indeed*, in *Works*, 5:498.

compared with his upon whose heart they have been acted! When such a man reads David's psalms or Paul's epistles, there he finds his own objections made and answered. "O," says he, "these holy men speak my very heart. Their doubts were mine, their troubles mine, and their experiences mine."... Experience is the best schoolmaster. O then, study your hearts, keep your hearts!

13

Furnish Your Hearts Richly with the Word

If you would thus keep your hearts as hath been persuaded, then furnish your hearts richly with the Word of God, which is their best preservative against sin. Keep the Word, and the Word will keep you. As the first receiving of the Word regenerated your hearts, so the keeping of the Word within you will preserve your hearts. "Let the word of Christ dwell in you richly" (Col. 3:16). Let it dwell, not tarry with you for a night, and let it dwell richly, or plentifully, in all that is of it, in its commands, promises, threats, in all that is in you, in your understandings, memories, consciences, affections, and then it will preserve your hearts (Ps. 119:11). It is the slipperiness of our hearts in reference to the Word that causes so many slips in our lives. Conscience cannot be urged, or awed, with forgotten truths. But keep it in the heart, and it will keep both heart and life upright. "The law of his God is in his heart: none of his steps shall slide" (Ps. 37:31); or if he do the Word will recover the straying heart again. We never lose our hearts till they have first lost the efficacious and powerful impressions of the Word.

From *A Saint Indeed*, in *Works*, 5:504–5.

Table of Contents to
Husbandy Spiritualized: The Heavenly Use of Earthly Things

Flavel used ordinary objects related to agriculture to convey spiritual truths to the farmers in his community.

14

Soul Work Is Preferred

No one will deny, but those are blessed pains,
which are attended with the richest gains.
Grant this, and then most clearly 'tis inferr'd,
soul work to all deserves to be preferr'd.
This is an unknown trade, oh, who can count,
to what the gains of godliness amount?
For one poor shilling, O, what risks some run?
Some toiling as in the fire, from sun to sun!
Where as one hour spent with God brings in
such heavenly treasures, that poor souls have been
inrich'd forever. Even as you see
a princess favorite upon the knee,
can in an hour's time more wealth obtain;
than all your lives by labor you can gain.
Prayer gains are great, and quick returns are made,
sure then the Christian drives the richest trade.
'Tis true, the hypocrite that never drove
a serious trade for heaven, may bankrupt prove;
But holy souls which mind, and closely ply
their business, greatly are enrich'd thereby.
The difference betwixt the one, and the other's best
by such a simile as this expressed.
As in a summer's day you often see,
the wanton butterfly and painful bee;

From *Husbandry Spiritualized*, in *Works*, 5:36–37.

on fragrant flowers fix, whence on doth strive
to bear his precious burden to the hive:
the other's pains no profit with it brings,
his time is spent, in painting of his wings.
When winter comes, the bee hath full supplies,
the other creeps into a hole and dies.
Like different events shall be betwixt
the painful saint, and lazy notionist.[1]

---

1. *notionist*: someone who knows the gospel but does not believe it

15

My Naughty Heart

A ship of greatest burden will obey
the rudder; he that sits at helm may sway,
and guide its motion: If the pilot please,
the ship bears up against both wind and seas.
My soul's the ship, affections are its sails,
conscience the rudder. Ah! But Lord what ails
my naughty heart, to shuffle in and out,
when its convictions bid it tack about?[1]
Temptations blow a counterblast, and drive
the vessel where they please, though conscience strive;
And by its strong persuasions, it would force,
my stubborn will to steer another course.
Lord, if I run this course, thy Word doth tell,
how quickly I must needs arrive at hell.
Then rectify my conscience, change my will,
fan in thy pleasant gales, my God, and fill,
all my affections; and let nothing carry,
my soul from its due course, or make it vary.
Then if the pilot's work Thou wouldst perform,
I should bear bravely up against the storm.

From *Navigation Spiritualized: A New Compass for Seamen*, in *The Works of John Flavel* (London: Banner of Truth, 1968), 5:233.

1. Flavel uses a play on words with "naughty," which sounds like "knotty." A tack knot is part of a harness that stops other ropes connected to it from sliding or "shuffling in and out" of the harness.

Seasons of the Heart

William Jenkyn (1613–1685)

A friend of Flavel, known for his commentary on Jude.
Soldiers once raided a service conducted by Flavel and
Jenkyn. While Flavel escaped, Jenkyn was captured.
Jenkyn was imprisoned at Newgate under
severe restriction and died there.

16

---•◦•---

Death of a Child

You cannot forget that in the years lately past, the Almighty visited my tabernacle with the rod and in one year cut off from it the root and the branch, the tender mother and the only son.[1] What the effects of those strokes, or rather of my own unmortified passions were, I have felt and you and others have heard. Surely I was a bullock unaccustomed to the yoke. Yea, I may say with them, "Remembering mine affliction and my misery, the wormwood and the gall. My soul hath them still in remembrance, and is humbled in me" (Lam. 3:19–20).

I dare not say that ever I felt my heart discontentedly rising and swelling against God. No, I could still justify Him, when I most sensibly smarted[2] by His hand. If He had plunged me into a sea of sorrow, yet I could say in all that sea of sorrow, there is not a drop of injustice. But it was the overheating and overacting of my fond and unmortified affections

From *A Token for Mourners, or The Advice of Christ to a Distressed Mother, Bewailing the Death of Her Dear and Only Son* (London: Banner of Truth, 1968), 5:604–5.

1. Flavel's wife, Joan Randall, along with the infant, died November 15, 1655, during childbirth. *Oxford Dictionary of National Biography*, s.v. "John Flavell."

2. *smarted*: to cause a sharp pain

and passions that made so sad impressions upon my body and cast me under those distempers that soon embittered all my remaining comforts to me.

It was my earnest desire, so soon as I had strength and opportunity for so great a journey to visit you, that so, if the Lord had pleased, I might both refresh and be refreshed by you, after all my sad and disconsolate days. And you cannot imagine what content and pleasure I projected in that visit; but it proved to us, as all other comforts of the same kind ordinarily do, more in expectation than in fruition. For how soon after our joyful meeting and embraces did the Lord overcast and darken our day, by sending death into your tabernacle, to take away the desire of your eyes with a stroke! To crop off that sweet and only bud from which we promised ourselves so much comfort. It is not my design to exasperate your troubles, but to heal them; and for that purpose have I sent you these papers, which I hope may be of use both to you and many others in your condition, since they are the after-fruits of my own troubles, things that I have not commended to you from another hand but which I have, in some measure, proved and tasted in my own trials.

But I will not hold you longer here. I have only a few things to desire for and from you, and I have done. That you will not be too hasty to get off the yoke which God hath put upon your neck. Remember when your child was in the womb, neither of you desired it should be delivered thence till God's appointed time was fully come, and now that you travail again with sorrow for its death, O desire not to be delivered from your sorrows one moment before

God's time for your deliverance is fully come also. "Let patience have its perfect work"; that comfort which comes in God's way and season will stick by you and do you good indeed (James 1:4).

17

Death of a Spouse

Madam, God has this day covered you with sables,[1] written bitter things against you, broken you with breach upon breach. Your sorrows need not to be excited, but regulated.... Hear you the rod, and who has appointed it; and, oh, that your soul may this day take in these necessary counsels and cautions, without which your afflictions cannot be sanctified to the advantage of your soul! And,

1. Learn from hence the vanity of the creature, the emptiness and nothingness of the best things here below.... Oh what a difference you will find between hope founded in Christ, comforts drawn out of the promises, and the flattering comforts and vain hopes founded in the creature whose breath is in its nostrils? It is time for you and for us all to wean off from this vain world, to mortify our fancies and affections to it and place them where they shall not be capable of disappointment.

2. Guard carefully, I beseech you, against those temptations that probably may accomplish this

From *A Sermon Preached for the Funeral of That Excellent and Religious Gentleman, John Upton, of Lupton, Esq.*, in *The Works of John Flavel* (London: Banner of Truth, 1968), 6:130–31.

1. *sables*: black clothing worn in mourning

affliction. It may be Satan will suggest to your heart what he once put into their lives: "What profit is it that we have kept his ordinance, and that we have walked mournfully before the LORD of hosts" (Mal. 3:14)? Where is the fruit of prayer? What good have I seen of fasting? What has religion availed? Do not prayerless and ungodly families thrive and prosper? Beware of this. Madam…remember the rewards of religion are not in this world…. All we must expect from religion is to save our souls by it.

3. Do not call the love of God into question to yourself, or yours, because of these severe strokes of God upon you and them…. Remember that it is but in the earth; here, or nowhere, God must chastise His children.

4. See that you maintain that holy course of religious exercises in your family and in your closet, where [your husband] walked so exemplarily before you. Let religion live, though he is dead; and convince the world, I pray you, that it was God's influence, and not your husband's only, that was the spring and principle of this holy course.

5. Strive not with your Maker, nor fret against the Lord under this irksome and painful dispensation. Remember, there is a woe hanging over this sin. "Woe unto him that striveth with his Maker" (Isa. 45:9–10).

IVLIANVS IMPERATOR
Ob impietatem ex sapiente insipiens
Ex numismate argenteo Barberinæ Bibliothecæ

Julian the Apostate (ca. 332–363)

18

Prosperity

Now then, the first case will be this, namely, how a Christian may keep his heart from pride and carnal security under the smiles of providence and constancy of creature comforts. There are seven choice helps to secure the heart from the dangerous snares of prosperity. The first is this:

1. To consider the dangerous ensnaring temptations attending a pleasant and prosperous condition; very few of those who live in the pleasures and prosperity of this world escape everlasting perdition (Matt. 19:24; 1 Cor. 1:26)....

2. It may keep us more humble and watchful in prosperity if we consider that among Christians many have been much the worse for it.... Outward gains are ordinarily attended with inward losses.... He indeed is rich in grace whose graces are not hindered by his riches....

3. Keep down your vain heart by this consideration, that God values no man a jot more for these things. God values no man by outward excellencies but by inward graces. They are the internal ornaments of the Spirit, which are of great price in God's eyes (1 Peter 3:4)....

From *A Saint Indeed*, in *Works*, 5:437–40.

4. Then, fourthly, consider how bitterly many persons have bewailed their folly when they came to die, that ever they set their hearts upon these things and heartily wished that they had never known them....

5. The heart may be kept humble, by considering what clogging nature earthly things are to a soul heartily engaged in the way to heaven. They shut out much of heaven from us at present, though they may not shut us out of heaven at last.... There was a serious truth in that atheistical scoff of Julian when he took away the Christians' estates and told them it was to make them fitter for the kingdom of heaven.[1]

6. Is your spirit, for all this, flatulent and lofty? Then urge upon it the consideration of that awful day of reckoning, wherein, according to our receipts of mercies, shall be our [accounting] for them.... You are but stewards, and your Lord will come to take an account of you....

7. It is a very humbling consideration that the mercies of God should work otherwise upon my spirit than they are used to doing upon the spirits of others to whom they come as sanctified mercies from the love of God.... The mercies of God have been melting mercies unto others, melting their souls in love to the God of their mercies....

---

1. Julian ruled as Roman emperor from AD 361–363. Originally accepting Christianity, he rejected it, instead desiring to restore paganism in Rome, thus receiving the name Julian the Apostate.

19

Adversity

The second special season in the life of a Christian requiring more than a common diligence to keep his heart is the time of adversity. When providence frowns upon you and blasts your outward comforts, then look to your hearts—keep them with all diligence from repining against God or fainting under His hand; for troubles, though sanctified, are troubles still.... Well then, the second case will be this: How can a Christian under great afflictions keep his heart from repining or desponding under the hand of God? Now there are nine special helps I shall here offer to keep your heart in this condition, and the first shall be this, to work upon your hearts this great truth.

1. That by these cross providences, God is faithfully pursuing the great design of electing love upon the souls of His people and orders all these afflictions as means sanctified to that end. Afflictions fall not out by casualty, but by counsel (Job 5:6; Eph. 1:11). By this counsel of God they are ordained as means of much spiritual good to saints (Isa. 27:9; Heb. 12:10; Rom. 8:28).... And sure, then, you have no reason to quarrel with, but rather to admire, that God should

From *A Saint Indeed*, in *Works*, 5:441–45.

concern Himself so much in your good, to use any means for the accomplishing of it (Phil. 3:11; James 1:2–3). My Father is about a design of love upon my soul, and do I well to be angry with Him?

2. Though God has reserved to Himself a liberty of afflicting His people, yet He has tied up His own hands by promise never to take away His lovingkindness from them. Can I look that Scripture in the face with a repining, discontented spirit (2 Sam. 7:14)?

3. It is of His marvelous efficacy to keep the heart from sinking under affliction, to call to mind that your own Father has the ordering of them. Not a creature moves hand or tongue against you, but by His permission.... The very consideration of His nature, a God of love, pity, and tender mercies, or of His relation to you as a father, husband, friend, might be security enough, if He had not spoken a word to quiet you in this case; and yet you have His word too (Jer. 25:6). You lie too near His heart to hurt you. Nothing grieves Him more than your groundless and unworthy suspicions of His designs do....

4. God respects you as much in a low, as in a big condition; and therefore it need not so much trouble you to be made low.... He manifests more of His love, grace, and tenderness in the time of affliction than prosperity....

5. And what if by the loss of outward comforts God will preserve your souls from the ruining power of temptations; sure then, you have little cause to sink your hearts by such sad thoughts about them.

6. It would much stay the heart under adversity to consider that God, by such humbling providences, may be accomplishing that for which you have long prayed and waited.... Would you be kept from sin? Lo, He has hedged up the way with thorns.... Would you have your heart to rest nowhere but in the bosom of God? What better way can you imagine providence should take to accomplish your desire than by pulling from under your head that soft pillow of creature-delights on which you rested before?

7. Again, it may stay your heart if you consider that in these troubles God is about that work, which if you did see the design of, your soul would rejoice.... Providence is like a curious piece of arras,[1] made up of a thousand shreds, which by themselves we know not what to make of, but put together and stitched up orderly, they represent a beautiful history to the eye. As God works all things according to the counsel of His own will, so that the counsel of God has ordained this as the best way to bring about your salvation....

8. Further, it would much conduce to the settlement of your hearts to consider that by fretting and discontent, you do yourselves more injury than all the afflictions you lie under could do.... Affliction is a pill, which, being wrapped up in patience and quiet submission, may be easily swallowed; but discontent chews the pill and so embitters the soul....

---

1. *arras*: tapestry

9. Lastly, if all this will not do, but your heart still refuses to be comforted or quieted, then consider one more.... Compare the condition you are now in (and are so much dissatisfied with) with that condition others are in and you deserve to be in....

20

The Church's Troubles

The third season calling for more than ordinary diligence to keep the heart is the time of Zion's troubles.... The third case that comes next to be spoken to is this: how public and tender hearts may be relieved and supported when they are overweighed with the burdensome sense of Zion's troubles.

1. Settle this great truth in your hearts, that no trouble befalls Zion but by the permission of Zion's God, and He permits nothing out of which He will not bring much good at last to His people.

2. Ponder this heart-supporting truth in reference to Zion's trouble: that however many troubles are upon her, yet her king is in her. What! Has the Lord forsaken His churches? Has He sold them into the enemy's hand?... The church's enemies are many and mighty, let that be granted, yet that argument with which Caleb and Joshua strove to raise their own hearts is of as much force now as it was then: "The LORD is with us: fear them not" (Num. 14:9)....

3. Ponder the great advantage attending the people of God in an afflicted condition. If a low and an afflicted state in this world is really best for the

From *A Saint Indeed*, in *Works*, 5:445–50.

church, then your dejections are not only irrational, but ungrateful.... If you reckon its glory to consist in its humility, faith, patience, and heavenly mindedness, no condition in the world abounds with advantages for these, as an afflicted condition does.... The power of godliness did never thrive better than in affliction and never ran lower than in times of greatest prosperity (Zeph. 3:12).

4. Take heed that you do not overlook the many precious mercies that the people of God enjoy amidst all their troubles.... Remember the church's true riches are laid out of the reach of all its enemies. They may make you poor, but not miserable....

5. Believe that however low the church is plunged under the waters of adversity, it shall assuredly rise again.

6. Record the famous instances of God's care and tenderness over His people in former straits.... Though we know not whence deliverance should arise, yet "the Lord knoweth how to deliver the godly out of temptations" (2 Peter 2:9)....

7. If you can fetch no comfort from any of the former arguments, then in the last place, try whether you cannot draw some comfort out of your very trouble.... This frame of spirit may afford you this argument, that if you are sensible of the church's troubles, Jesus Christ is much more sensible of and solicitous about it than you can be, and He will have an eye of favor upon those that mourn for it (Isa. 57:18).

21

Fear and Danger

The fourth special season of expressing our utmost diligence in keeping our hearts is the time of danger and public distraction: in such times the best hearts are but too apt to be surprised by slavish fear. It is not easy to secure the heart against distractions in times of common distraction.... Well, then, the fourth case will be this: how a Christian may keep his heart from distracting and tormenting fears in times of great and threatening dangers....

Remember that this God in whose hand all the creatures are is your Father and is much more tender over you than you are, or can be, over yourselves (Zech. 2:8).... Consider Christ first as the king and supreme lord over the providential kingdom, and then as your head, husband, and friend, and you will quickly say, "Return unto thy rest, O my soul" (Ps. 116:7)....

Urge upon your hearts the express prohibitions of Christ in this case, and let your hearts stand in awe of the violations of them. He has charged you not to fear (Luke 21:9; Phil. 1:28; Matt. 10:26–31).... I think the command of Christ should have as much power to calm, as the voice of a poor worm to terrify, your heart (Isa. 51:12–13)....

From *A Saint Indeed*, in *Works*, 5:450–57.

Remember how much needless trouble your vain fears have brought upon you formerly and how you have disquieted yourselves to no purpose....

Consult the many precious promises that are written for your support and comfort in all dangers. These are your refuges to which you may flee and be safe when the arrows of danger fly by night and destruction lays waste at noonday (Ps. 91:5–6). There are particular promises suited to particular cases and exigencies, and there are general promises reaching all cases and conditions (Rom. 8:28; Eccl. 8:12; 2 Chron. 20:29; Gen. 32:12)....

Quiet your trembling hearts by recording and consulting your past experiences of the care and faithfulness of God in former distresses. These experiences are food for your faith in a wilderness condition (Ps. 74:14)....

Learn to quench all slavish creature fears in the reverential fear of God. This is a cure by diversion. It is a rare piece of Christian wisdom to turn those passions of the soul that most predominate into spiritual channels, to turn...natural fear into a holy dread and awe of God. This method of cure Christ prescribes (Matt. 10:28; Isa. 8:12–13)....

Pour out those fears to God in prayer that the devil and your own unbelief pour in upon you in times of danger. Prayer is the best outlet to fear.

22

---◆◆(●)◆◆---

In Times of Need

The fifth season to exert this diligence in keeping the heart is the time of [dire] straits and outward pinching wants. Although at such times we should complain to God, and not of God.... The fifth case therefore shall be this: how a Christian may keep his heart from distrusting God or repining against Him when outward wants are either felt or feared....

1. Consider that if God reduce you to straits and necessities, yet He deals no otherwise therein with you than He has with some of the choicest and holiest men that ever lived...Paul...David...even the Son of God, who is the heir of all things, and by whom the worlds were made, yet sometime would have been glad of anything, having nothing to eat (1 Cor. 4:11; 1 Sam. 25:8; Heb. 1:2; Mark 11:12)....

2. Consider if God leave you not in this necessitous condition without a promise, you have no reason to repine or despond under it.... Now God has left many sweet promises for the faith of His poor people to feed on in this condition (Pss. 34:9–10; 33:18–19; 48:11; Rom. 8:32; Isa. 41:17). Having therefore these promises, why should not your mistrustful hearts

From *A Saint Indeed*, in *Works*, 5:465–68.

conclude like David's, "The LORD is my shepherd; I shall not want" (Psalm 23:1)...?

3. Consider if it is bad now, it might have been worse if God had denied you the comforts of this life. He might have denied you Christ, peace, and pardon also, and then your case had been woeful indeed....

4. Consider that this affliction, though great, is not such an affliction but God has far greater with which He chastises the dearly beloved of His soul in this world, and should He remove this and inflict those, you would account your present state a very comfortable state, and bless God to be as now you are.

5. Consider if it be bad now, it will be better shortly.... Desponding soul, does it become a man or woman travailing upon the road to that heavenly city, and almost arrived there, within a few days' journey of his Father's house, where all his wants shall be supplied, to take on thus about a little meat, drink, or clothes, which he fears he shall want by the way?

6. Consider does it become children of such a Father to distrust His all-sufficiency or repine against any of His dispensations?

7. Consider your poverty is not your sin, but your affliction only. If by sinful means you have brought it upon yourselves and if it is but as affliction, it may be borne the easier for this.... And thus I have showed you how to keep your hearts from the temptations and dangers attending a poor and low condition in the world, when want pinches and the heart begins to sink, then improve and bless God for these helps to keep it.

23

Distraction during Religious Duties

The sixth season of expressing this diligence in keeping the heart is the season of duty. When we draw nigh to God in public, private, or secret duties, then it is time to look to the heart. For the vanity of the heart seldom discovers itself more than at such times....

1. Sequester yourselves from all earthly employments and set apart some time for solemn preparation to meet God in duty. You cannot come reeking hot out of the world into God's presence, but you will find a tang of it in your duties.... O when you go to God in any duty, take your heart aside and say, "O my soul! I am now addressing myself to the greatest work that ever a creature was employed about. I am going into the awful presence of God about business of everlasting moment. Oh, my soul, I leave trifling now, be composed, watchful, serious, this is no common work. It is God-work, soul-work, eternity work. I am now going forth bearing seed, which will bring forth fruit to life or death in the world to come." Pause a while upon your sins, wants, troubles; keep your thoughts a while in these before you address yourself to duty (Pss. 39:3–4; 45:1).

From *A Saint Indeed*, in *Works*, 5:463–68.

2. Having composed your heart by previous meditation presently set a guard upon your senses. How often are poor Christians in danger of losing the eyes of their mind by those of their body, for this Job covenanted with his senses, and David prayed (Job 31:1; Ps. 119:37)....

3. Beg of God a mortified fancy[1]; a working fancy, however much it be extolled among men, is a great snare to the soul [if] imaginations are not first cast down. It is impossible [then] that every thought of the heart should be brought into obedience to Christ (2 Cor. 10:5)....

4. If you would keep your heart from these vain excursions, realize for yourself by faith the holy and awful presence of God in duties. If the presence of a grave man will compose us to seriousness, how much more the presence of a holy God? Do you think your soul would dare to be so garish and light if the sense of a divine eye were upon it? Remember the place where you are is the place of His feet (Isa. 60:13).... Present God thus before yourself, and your vain heart will quickly be reduced to a more serious frame.

5. Maintain a praying frame of heart in the intervals of duty. What is the reason our hearts are so dull, careless, and wandering when we come to hear or pray, but because there have been such long intermissions in our communion with God, by reason whereof the heart is out of a praying frame. If that spiritual warmth, those holy impressions we carry from God in one duty, were but preserved to kindle

---

1. *fancy*: an imagination

another duty, it would be of marvelous advantage to keep the heart intent and serious with God....

6. Endeavor to image and raise your affections to God in duty if you would have your distractions cured.... The affections command the thoughts to go after them.... The soul could dwell day and night upon its knees when once its delights, loves, and desires are engaged. What's the reason your hearts are so shuffling, especially in secret duties? Why are you ready to be gone almost as soon as you are come into the presence of God, but because your affections are not engaged?

7. Mourn over the matter to God, and call in assistance from heaven, when vain thoughts assault your heart in duty.... Never slight wandering thoughts in duty as small matters. Follow every vain thought with a deep sigh [and] turn to God with such words as these: "Lord, I came hither to speak with Thee, and here a busy devil and a vain heart conspiring together have set upon me.... Help me, my God. This once do but display Thy glory before my eyes, and my heart shall quickly be recovered."

8. Look upon the success and sweetness of your duties as very much depending upon the keeping of your heart close with God in them. These two things, the success, and sweetness of duty, are as dear to a Christian as his two eyes, and both of these must necessarily be lost if the heart is lost in duty (Job 35:13; Jer. 29:13). Well then, when you find your heart under the power of deadness and distraction, say to your soul, "O what do I lose by a careless heart

now! My praying times are the choicest parts, the golden spots of all my time. Could I but get up this heart with God, I might now obtain such mercies as would be matter for a song to all eternity."

9. Look upon it as a great discovery of the sincerity or hypocrisy of your hearts according as you find them careful or careless in this matter. Nothing will startle an upright heart more than this: "What, shall I give way to a customary wandering of heart from God? Shall the spot of the hypocrite appear upon my soul?... O never let me be satisfied with empty duties! Never let me take my leave of a duty, until 'mine eyes have seen the King, the LORD of hosts'" (Isa. 6:5).

10. Lastly, it will be of special use to keep your heart with God in duties, to consider what influence all your duties have into your eternity. These are your seed times, and what you sow in your duties in this world you must look to read the fruit of it in another world.... "O, my soul, answer seriously, would you be willing to reap the fruit of vanity in the world to come?"

24

Abuse from Others

The seventh season calling for more than common diligence to keep the heart is when we receive injuries and abuses from men; such is the depravity and corruption of man in his collapsed state.... Now when we are thus abused and wronged, it is hard to keep the heart from revengeful motions to make it meek and quiet, to commit the cause to Him who judges righteously, to exercise no other affection but pity toward those who abuse us. Surely the spirit that is in us lusts to revenge, but it must not be so. You have choice helps in the gospel to keep down your hearts from such sinful motions against your enemies and to sweeten your embittered spirits. The seventh case therefore shall be this: how a Christian may keep his heart from revengeful motions, under the greatest injuries and abuses from men.

The gospel allows us a liberty to vindicate our innocence and assert our rights, but not to vent our corruptions and invade God's right. When therefore you find your heart begin to be inflamed by revengeful motions, presently apply the following remedies, and the first is this.

Urge upon your heart the severe prohibitions of revenge by the law of God. Remember that this

From *A Saint Indeed*, in *Works*, 5:468–73.

King Charles II (1630–1685)

Charles II reigned over England from 1660 to 1685.
During his reign, persecution and mistreatment
of the Puritans was common.

is forbidden fruit, however pleasing and luscious it is to our vitiated appetites. O, but God says, the effects thereof shall be bitter. How plainly has God interdicted this flesh-pleasing sin (Prov. 20:22; 24:29; 25:21; Rom. 12:17–19)?

Well, then, awe your hearts with the authority of God in these Scriptures, and when carnal reason says, "My enemy deserves to be hated," let conscience reply, "But does God deserve to be disobeyed?"

Set before your eyes the most eminent patterns of meekness and forgiveness, that your souls may fall in love with it.... Never did any suffer more and greater abuses from men than Christ did, and never did any carry it more peaceably and forgivingly (Isa. 53:7). This pattern the apostle sets before you for your imitation (1 Peter 2:21–23). To be of a meek, forgiving spirit is Christ-like, God-like (Matt. 5:45). How eminently also did this Spirit of Christ rest upon His apostles. Never were there such men upon earth for true excellency of spirit. None were ever abused more or suffered their abuses better (1 Cor. 4:12–13)....

Keep down your heart by this consideration, that by revenge you can only satisfy a lust, but by forgiveness you shall conquer a lust. Suppose by revenge you should destroy one enemy, I will show you how by forgiving you shall conquer three: your own lusts, the devil's temptation, and your enemy's heart—and is not this a more glorious conquest?

Seriously propound this question to your own heart. Have I gotten any good from the wrong and injuries received, or have I not? What, can you not find a heart to forgive one that has been instrumental of so much good to you? That's strange! When though they meant it for evil, yet if God have turned it to good (Gen. 50:20), you have no more reason to rage against the instrument....

It is of excellent use to keep the heart from revenge, to look up and eye the First Cause by which all our troubles are ordered.... But though it does not fall under His approving, yet it does under His permitting will, and there is a great argument for quiet submission in that. He has not only the permitting but also the ordering of all those troubles. If we were to see more of a holy God, we would show less of a corrupt nature in such trials.

Consider how you daily wrong God, and you will not be so easily inflamed with revenge against others who have wronged you.... It is impossible we can be cruel to others, except we forget how kind Christ has been to us. Those that have found mercy should show mercy. If kindness cannot work, I think fear should (Matt. 6:15).

Lastly, let the consideration of the day of the Lord, which draws nigh, withhold your hearts from anticipating it by acts of revenge (James 5:7–9). This text affords three arguments against revenge: the Lord's near approach; the example of the husbandman's[1] patience; the danger we draw upon ourselves by anticipating God's judgment. "Vengeance is Mine," says the Lord. He will distribute justice more equally and impartially than you can. They that believe they have a God to right them will not so much wrong themselves as to avenge their own wrongs.[2]

---

1. *husbandman*: farmer

25

------- ⇒ »‹(•)›« ⇐ -------

Anger

The next season in which we are in danger of losing our hearts is when we meet with great crosses and provocations. Then sinful passion is apt to transport the heart.... The eighth case therefore is this: how the heart may be kept meek and patient under great crosses and provocations....

1. Get low and humble thoughts of yourselves, and then you will have meek spirits and peaceable deportments toward others.... When we overrate ourselves, then we think we are unworthily treated by others, and that provokes; and here (by the way) take notice of one great benefit of acquaintance with your own hearts, even the meekening and calming of our spirits. Christian, I think you should know so much by yourself that it is impossible any should lay you lower or have baser thoughts of you than you have of yourself.... O get more humility, and that will bring you more peace.

2. Be often sweetening your spirit in communion with God, and they will not easily be embittered with wrath toward men. A quiet conscience never produced an unquiet conversation!... This is so

From *A Saint Indeed*, in *Works*, 5:473–77.

1. *conversation*: life

effectual a remedy against passion that I dare almost venture a Christian of a hasty nature to make long-suffering a sign of communion with God....

3. Get due apprehensions of the evil nature and effects of sinful anger.... The effects of it also are very sad. It grieves the Spirit of God (Eph. 4:30).... It gives advantage to the devil (Eph. 4:26–27).... It dis-tunes the spirit for duty (1 Peter 3:7).... It disparages the Christian religion.

4. Consider how sweet a thing it is to a Christian to conquer his corruptions and carry away the spoils of them. "He that is slow to anger is better than the mighty; and he that ruleth his spirit than he that taketh a city" (Prov. 16:32)....

5. Shame yourselves by setting before you those eminent patterns that have been most excellent for meekness. Above all, compare your spirits with the Spirit of Christ (Matt. 11:29). Christ was meek and lowly, but I am proud and passionate. It was the high commendation of Moses (Num. 12:3)....

6. Lastly, avoid all irritating occasions.... Do not pray and resolve against it, but get as far as you can out of the way of it. It is true spiritual valor to run as fast and as far as we can out of sin's way. If you can but avoid anger in its first rise there is no great fear of it afterwards, for it is not with this sin as it is with other sins. Other sins grow to their full strength by degrees—their first motions are the weakest; but this sin is born in its full strength. It is strongest at first. Withstand it then, and it falls before you.

26

Temptation, Part 1

The ninth season of exerting our greatest diligence is the critical hour of temptation, wherein Satan lays close siege to the fort royal of a Christian's heart and often surprises it for want of watchfulness. To keep your heart now is no less a mercy than a duty. Few Christians are so well skilled in detecting the fallacies and retorting the arguments by which Satan uses to draw them to sin as to come off late in those encounters (Mark 14:38).... The ninth case therefore shall be this: how a Christian, when strongly solicited by the devil to sin, may keep his heart from yielding to the temptation.

The first argument is drawn from the pleasure of sin. "O," says Satan, "here is pleasure to be enjoyed." Temptation comes with a smiling countenance and charming voice. What, are you so phlegmatic and dull a soul that you do not feel the powerful charms of pleasure? Who can withhold himself from such delight?

Now your heart may be kept from the danger of this temptation by retorting this argument of pleasure upon the tempter, which is done two ways. First, "You tell me, Satan, that sin is pleasant. It may

From *A Saint Indeed*, in *Works*, 5:477–79.

be, but are the grips of consciences and the flames of hell so too? If so, why did Peter weep so bitterly (Matt. 26:75)? Why did David cry out of broken bones (Ps. 51:8)? I hear what you say about the pleasure of sin, and I have read what David has said of the terrible effects of sin in his psalm, to bring to remembrance (Psalm 38). Here I see the true face of sin. If I yield to your temptation, I must either feel these pangs of conscience or the flames of hell." Second, "Why do you speak of the pleasure of sin, when by experience I know there is more true pleasure in mortification than can be in the commission of sin? O, how sweet it is to please God, to obey conscience, to preserve inward peace, to be able to say in this trial I have discovered the sincerity of my heart. Now I know I fear the Lord. Now I see that I truly hate sin. Has sin any such delight as this?" This will choke that temptation.

The second argument is drawn from the secrecy of sin. "O," Satan says, "this sin will never disgrace you abroad; none shall know it." This argument may be retorted and the heart secured thus: "You say none shall know of it, but Satan, can you find a place void of the divine presence for me to sin in? Thus Job secured his heart from this temptation: 'Doth not he see my ways, and count all my steps?' (Job 31:4). Therefore he makes a covenant with his eyes (Job 31:1). After the same manner Solomon teaches us to retort this temptation (Prov. 5:20–21). What if I hide it from the eyes of all the world for the present, I cannot hide it from God; and the time is at hand, when all the world shall know it too, for the Word assures me

that what is done now in secret shall be proclaimed
as upon the housetop (Luke 8:17). Besides, is not my
conscience as a thousand witnesses?"

The third argument by which Satan tempts to sin is
taken from the gain and profit arising out of it. "Why
so nice and scrupulous? Just stretch your conscience
a little and you can make yourself. Now is your
opportunity." The heart may be kept from falling
into this dangerous snare by retorting the temptation
thus: " 'For what is a man profited, if he shall gain the
whole world, and lose his own soul? Or what shall a
man give in exchange for his soul?' (Matt. 16:26). O
my soul, my precious soul! Shall I hazard you for all
the good that is in this world? There is an immortal
spirit dwelling in this fleshly tabernacle of more
value than all earthly things that must live to all eternity when this world shall lie in white ashes. A soul
for which Jesus Christ shed His precious and invaluable blood: I was sent into this world to provide for
this soul. Indeed, God has also committed to me the
care of my body, but (as one happily expresses it)[1]
with this difference. A master commits two things to
a servant, the child and the child's clothes. Will the
master thank the servant if, he please, I have kept the
clothes, but I have neglected the life of the child?"

---

1. Here Flavel references a work from the Exeter minister Lewis
Stuckley, *A Gospel-Glasse, or, A Call from Heaven to Sinners and Saints*
(London, 1667), 3.

27

Temptation, Part 2

The fourth argument is drawn from the smallness of the sin. It is but a little one, a small matter, a trifle. Who should stand upon such niceties? This argument may be retorted three ways.

1. But is the majesty of heaven a little one too? If I commit this sin, I must offend and wrong a great God (Isa. 40:15–22).

2. Is there any little hell to torment little sinners in? Are not the least sinners there filled with the fullness of wrath? O, there is great wrath treasured up for such as the world counts little sinners.

3. The less the sin, the less the inducement to commit it. What, shall I break with God for a trifle? Destroy my peace, wound my conscience, grieve the Spirit, and all this for nothing? Oh what madness is this?

A fifth argument is drawn from the grace of God and hopes of pardon. Come, God will pass by this as an infirmity; He will not be extreme to mark it. But stay, my heart.

Where do I find a promise of mercy to presumptuous sinners? Indeed, for involuntary surprises,

From *A Saint Indeed*, in *Works*, 5:479–80.

unavoidable, and lamented infirmities, there is a pardon, of course. But where is the promise to a daring sinner who sins upon a presumption of pardon? Pause awhile, my soul, upon this Scripture: "And if any soul sin through ignorance, then he shall bring a she goat of the first year for a sin offering.... But the soul that doeth ought presumptuously, whether he be born in the land, or a stranger, the same reproacheth the LORD; and that soul shall be cut off from among his people" (Num. 15:27–30).

If God be a God of so much mercy, how can I abuse so good a God? Shall I take so glorious an attribute as the mercy of God is and abuse it unto sin? Shall I wrong Him because He is good? Or should not rather the goodness of God lead me to repentance (Rom. 2:4)? "There is forgiveness with thee, that thou mayest be feared" (Ps. 130:4).

Lastly [argument six], sometimes Satan encourages to sin from the examples of good and holy men. So-and-so has sinned and been restored. Therefore this may consist with grace, and you are saved nevertheless. The danger of this temptation is avoided, and the heart secured, by retorting the argument these three ways.

1. Though good men may commit the same sin materially that I am tempted to, yet did ever any good man venture to sin upon such a ground and encouragement as this?

2. Did God record these examples for my imitation, or for my warning? Are they not set up as seamarks, that I might avoid the rocks upon which they split?

"Now these were our examples, to the intent we should not lust after evil things, as they also lusted" (1 Cor. 10:6).

3. Am I willing to feel what they felt for sin? O, I dare not follow them in the ways of sin…lest God should plunge me into the deeps of horror into which He cast them.

28

—◦—«(•)»—◦—

Spiritual Darkness

The tenth special season to keep the heart with all diligence is the time of spiritual darkness and doubting.... The tenth case then will be this: how the people of God, in dark and doubting seasons, may keep their hearts from entertaining such sad conclusions about their estates and destroy their peace and unfit them for their duty....

1. That every working and appearance of hypocrisy does not presently prove the person in whom it is to be a hypocrite. You must carefully distinguish between the presence and predominance of hypocrisy. There are remains of deceitfulness in the best hearts; David and Peter had sad experience of it, yet the standing frame and general bent of their hearts was upright. It did not denominate them hypocrites.

2. That we ought as well to bear what can be said for us, as against us. It is the sin of upright hearts sometimes to use an over-rigid and merciless severity against themselves. They do not indifferently consider the case of their own souls.... It is the damning sin of the self-flattering hypocrite to make his condition better than it is. And it is the sin and folly of some upright ones to make their condition worse

From *A Saint Indeed*, in *Works*, 5:480–82.

than indeed it is. Why should you be such enemies to your own peace? To read over the evidences of God's love to your souls as a man does a book that he intends to refute? Why do you study to find evasions, to turn off these comforts that are due to you?

3. That many a saint has charged and condemned himself for that which God will never charge him with or condemn him for....

4. Everything that is a ground of grief to the people of God is not a sufficient ground of questioning their sincerity. There are many more things to trouble you than there are to stumble you. If upon every slip and failing through infirmity you should question all that ever was wrought upon you, your life must be made up of doubtings and fears. You can never attain a settled peace or live that life of praise and thankfulness the gospel calls for.

5. The soul is not at all times fit to pass judgment upon its own condition. To be sure in the dark day of desertion, when the soul is benighted, and in the stormy day of temptation, when the soul is in a hurry—these are times utterly unfit to judge its estate. Examine your hearts upon your beds, and be still (Ps. 4:4). This is rather a season for watching and resisting than for judging and determining.

6. That every breach of peace with God is not a breach of covenant with God. A wife may have many weaknesses and failings and often grieves and displeases her husband, yet in the main, she is faithful and truly loves him. These failings may cause him to alter his behavior, but not to withdraw his love or

deny his relation. "Turn, O back-sliding children…
for I am married unto you" (Jer. 3:14).

7. Lastly, whatever our sin or trouble is, it should
rather drive us to God than from God. "Pardon mine
iniquity; for it is great" (Ps. 25:11). Suppose it is true
that you have sinned in some way, that you are thus
long and sadly deserted, yet it is a false inference that
therefore you should be discouraged, as if there were
no help for you in your God.

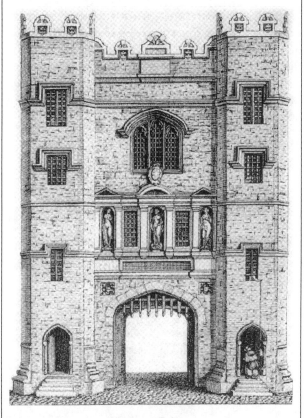

Newgate Prison

Imprisonment was a constant threat for nonconformists.
Flavel's parents were imprisoned at Newgate in 1665,
where they caught the plague and died upon their release.

29

━━━━ ➤•(•)•➤ ━━━━

Suffering for Religion

The eleventh special season calling for this diligence to keep your hearts is when sufferings for religion come to an height, then look to your hearts (Matt. 24:8–10; Mic. 7:5–6; 2 Tim. 2:19; 4:16; Heb. 11:37; 12:4; Jer. 17:17).... How the heart may be kept from relapsing under the greatest sufferings for religion? If the bitterness of sufferings at any time causes your soul to distaste the way of God and take up thoughts of forsaking it, stay your heart under that temptation by propounding these eight questions solemnly to it.

1. What reproach and dishonor shall I pour upon Christ and religion by deserting Him at such a time as this?

2. Dare I violate my conscience to save my flesh? Who shall comfort me when conscience wounds me?

3. Is not the public interest of Christ and religion infinitely more than any private interest of my own?

4. Did Jesus Christ serve me so, when, for my sake, He exposed Himself to far greater sufferings than can be before me? His sufferings were great indeed; He suffered from all hands, in all His offices, in every member, not only in His body but in His soul.

From *A Saint Indeed*, in *Works*, 5:487–89.

Yea, the sufferings of His soul were the very soul of His sufferings…. Did Christ bear such a burden for me with unbroken patience and constancy, and shall I shrink back from momentary and light afflictions for Him?

5. Is not eternal life worth the suffering of a moment's pain? If I suffer with Him, I shall reign with Him (2 Tim. 2:12).

6. Can I so easily cast off the society and company of the saints and give the right hand of fellowship to the wicked?

7. Have I seriously considered the terrible Scripture comminations[1] against backsliders (Jer. 5:6; Heb. 10:26–27, 38)?

8. Can I look Christ in the face at the day of judgment if I desert Him now? "Whosoever therefore shall be ashamed of me and of my words in this adulterous and sinful generation; of him also shall the Son of man be ashamed, when he cometh in the glory of his Father with the holy angels" (Mark 8:38).

---

1. *comminations*: threats; denunciations

30

Willingness to Die

The twelfth season of looking diligently to our hearts and keeping them with greatest care is the time of sickness...[and a] shrinking from death [, a loathing] to depart.... Well then, the last case shall be this: how the people of God in times of sickness may get their hearts loose from all earthly engagements and persuade them into a willingness to die. And there are seven arguments that I will urge upon the people of God at such a time as this, to make them cheerfully entertain the messengers of death and die as well as live like saints; and the first is this.

1. The harmlessness of death to the people of God. Though it keeps its dart, it hath lost its sting.... It has left and lost its sting in the sides of Christ: "O death, where is thy sting?" (1 Cor. 15:55).

2. Your heart may be kept from shrinking back at [death] by considering the necessity of death, in order to the full fruition of God. Whether you are willing to die or not, I assure you there is no other way to obtain the full satisfaction of your soul and complete its happiness. Until the hand of death does you the kind office of drawing aside the curtain of

From *A Saint Indeed*, in *Works*, 5:490–93.

flesh, your soul cannot see God. This animal life[1] stands between him and you (2 Cor. 5:6). Your body must be refined and cast into a new mold, else that new wine of heavenly glory would break it.... Who would not be willing to die for a full sight and enjoyment of God?... Most men need patience to die, but a saint that understands what death admits him to should rather need patience to live. I think he should often look out and listen on a deathbed for his Lord's coming, and when he receives the news of His approaching change should say, "The voice of my beloved! behold, he cometh leaping upon the mountains, skipping upon the hills" (Song 2:8)....

3. Another argument persuading to this willingness is the immediate succession of a more excellent and glorious life. It is only a wink, and you shall see God. Your happiness shall not be deferred till the resurrection, but as soon as the body is dead the gracious soul is swallowed up in life (Rom. 8:10–11)....

4. Farther, it may much conduce to your willingness to die to consider that by death God oftentimes hides His people out of the way of all temptations and troubles upon earth (Rev. 14:13)....

5. If yet your heart hangs back, consider the great advantage you will have by death above all that ever you enjoyed on earth. For your communion with God, the time of perfecting that is now come. Your soul shall shortly stand before the face of God and have the immediate emanations and beamings forth of His glory upon it....

---

1. *animal life*: earthly life

6. If all this will not do, consider what heavy burdens death will ease your shoulders of.... Death is the best physician; it will cure you of all diseases at once....

7. If still you linger like Lot in Sodom, then lastly examine all the pleas and pretences for a longer time on earth. Why are you unwilling to die?

SECTION FOUR

Discerning the Heart

Jonathan Edwards (1703–1758)

Edwards appreciated the experiential emphasis
of the Puritans and referenced Flavel many times
in *A Treatise Concerning Religious Affections*.

31

The Aim of Our Hearts

The designs and true levels and aims of men's hearts in duty will tell them what they are. A hypocrite aims low: "They have not cried unto me with their heart, when they howled upon their beds; they assembled themselves for corn and wine, and they rebel against me" (Hos. 7:14). It is not for Christ and pardon, for mortification and holiness, but for corn and wine. Thus they make a market of religion. All their ends in duty are carnal, natural, or legal. It is either to accommodate their carnal ends or satisfy their consciences, and so their duties are performed as a sin offering to God.

But an upright heart has very high and pure aims in duty: the desire of their soul is to God (Isa. 26:8); their soul follows hard after God (Ps. 63:8). "One thing have I desired of the LORD, that will I seek after; that I might dwell in the house of the LORD all the days of my life, to behold the beauty of the LORD, and to enquire in his temple" (Ps. 27:4).

The engagements of men's hearts to God in duties will tell them what they are. The hypocrite takes little heed to his heart (Isa. 29:13). They are not

---

From *The Touchstone of Sincerity: or, The Signs of Grace, and Symptoms of Hypocrisy,* in *The Works of John Flavel* (London: Banner of Truth, 1968), 5:566–68.

afflicted really for the hardness, deadness, unbelief, and wanderings of their hearts in duty as upright ones are. Nor do they engage their hearts and labor to get them up with God in duty as His people do. "I intreated thy favour with my whole heart," says David (Ps. 119:58). [God's people] are not pleased in duty till they feel their hearts stand toward God like a bow in its full bent. I say not it is always so with them. What would they give that it might be so! But surely if their souls in duty be empty of God, they are filled with trouble and sorrow.

The conscience men make of secret as well as of public duties will tell them what their hearts and graces are, true or false. A vain professor is curious in the former and either negligent, or at best formal, in the latter, for he finds no inducements of honor, applause, or ostentation of gifts externally moving him to them. Nor does he have any experience of the sweetness and benefit of such duties internally to allure and engage his soul to them. The hypocrite therefore is not for the closet, but the synagogue (Matt. 6:5–6)....

But now a truly gracious soul cannot long subsist without secret prayer. It is true—there is not always an equal freedom and delight, a like enlargement and comfort in those retirements, but yet he cannot be without them. He finds the want of his secret [duties] in his public duties. If he and his God have not met in secret and had some communion in the morning, he sensibly finds it in the deadness and unprofitableness of his heart and life all the day after.

The spirituality of our duties tries the sincerity of our graces: an unregenerate heart is carnal while engaged in duties that are spiritual.... O my friends, it is not enough that the object of your duties is spiritual, that they respect a holy God or that the matter is spiritual, that you be conversant about holy things; but that the frame of your heart must be spiritual, a heavenly temper of soul is necessary. And what are the most heavenly duties without it?

32

---◆━◗(◉)◖━◆---

The Hypocrite's
Abstinence from Sin

The grounds and motives of our abstinence do very clearly manifest the state of our souls, what they are in the regenerate and unregenerate....

First, that an unsound and unrenewed heart may abstain from one sin because it is contrary to and inconsistent with another sin...prodigality and covetousness, hypocrisy and profaneness. These oppose each other, not for mutual destruction, as sin and grace do, but for superiority, each contending for the throne and sometimes taking it by turns. It is with such persons as with that possessed man (Matt. 17:15) whom the spirit cast sometimes into the fire, sometimes into the water. Or, if one subdues the other, yet the heart is also subdued to the vassalage of that lust that is uppermost in the soul.

Secondly, an unrenewed soul may be kept from the commission of some sin, not because there is a principle of grace within him, but because of some providential constraints without him or upon him. For it often falls out that when men have conceived sin and are ready to execute it, providence claps on the fetters of restraint and hinders them from doing

---

From *Touchstone of Sincerity*, in *Works*, 5:551–53.

so. This was the case of Abimelech (Gen. 20:6 and 17 compared)....

Thirdly, an unsound heart may not commit some sins, not because he truly hates them, but because his constitution inclines him not to them. These men are rather beholden to a good temper of body than a gracious temper of soul....

Fourthly, a graceless heart may be restrained from sin by the force of education and principles of morality that were instilled into it. Thus Jehoash was restrained from sin (2 Kings 12:2). The fear of a parent or master will do a great deal more with some in this case than the fear of God. The influences of strict education nips off the [excesses] of budding vice. The way we are taught when young, we keep when old. This is the influence of man upon man, not the influence of the regenerating Spirit upon men.

Fifthly, a graceless heart may be kept in some sins by the fear of events, both in this world and that to come. Sin that is followed with infamy and reproach among men may on this ground be forborne, not because God hath forbidden it but because human laws will punish it, and the sober world will brand us for it. And some look farther, to the punishment of sin in hell. They are not afraid to sin, but they are afraid to burn....

And thus you see some of the grounds on which carnal men are restrained: and in this the children of the devil are manifest (1 John 3:10).

33

The Saint's Abstinence from Sin

But there are grounds of abstinence from sin, by which "the children of God are manifest" (1 John 3:10), and such are these that follow.

First, a sincere heart dares not sin because of the eye and fear of God that is on him; so you find it in Job 31:1 and 4. He dared not allow his thoughts to sin because he lived under the awe of God's eye. Nehemiah dared not do as former governors had done, though an opportunity presented to enrich himself, "because of the fear of God" (Neh. 5:15)....

Secondly, as the fear of God, so the love of God is a principle of restraint from sin to the soul that is upright. This kept back Joseph from sin: "How can I do this great wickedness, and sin against God?" (Gen. 39:9).... So Psalm 97:10, "Ye that love the LORD, hate evil." Love will cry out in the hour of temptation, "Is this your kindness to your friend? Do you requite the Lord in this way for all His kindness?"

Thirdly, as the love of God, so the intrinsic evil and filthiness that is in sin keeps back the gracious soul from it: "Abhor that which is evil"; hate it as hell itself (Rom. 12:9)....

From *Touchstone of Sincerity,* in *Works,* 5:553–54.

Fourthly, the renewed nature of a saint restrains him from sin. "The spirit lusts against the flesh, so that you cannot do the thing you would" (Gal. 5:17).... Beloved, this is a very remarkable thing in the experience of all renewed men, that, upon the renovation of men's principles, their delights and their aversions and loathings are laid quite cross and opposite to what they were before. In their carnal state, vain company and sinful exercises were their delight. To be separated from these and tied to prayer, meditation, heavenly discourse, and company, O what a bondage would that have been! Now to be tied to such carnal society and restrained from such duties of godliness and the society of the godly become a much sorer bondage to the soul.

Fifthly, experience of the bitterness of sin is a restraint to a gracious heart. They that have had so many sick days and sorrowful nights for sin as they have had are loath to taste that wormwood and gall again, which their soul still remembers in "that ye sorrowed after a godly sort, what carefulness it wrought" (2 Cor. 7:11). He would not grapple with those inward troubles again. He would not have the cheerful light of God's countenance eclipsed again for all, and much more than all, the pleasures that are in sin.

Sixthly, the consideration of the sufferings of Christ for sin powerfully withholds a gracious soul from the commission of it. "Our old man is crucified with him, that the body of sin might be destroyed, that henceforth we should not serve sin" (Rom. 6:6). Were there a knife or sword in the house that had been thrust through the heart of your father would you even endure the sight of it? Sin was the sword that pierced Christ, and so the death of Christ becomes the death of sin in His people. Thus the children of God and the children of the devil are manifest in the principles and reasons of their abstinence from sin.

34

The Hypocrite's Hatred of Sin

[The children of God and the devil] are also manifested by their hatred of sin. This puts a clear distinction between them, for no false or unregenerate heart can hate sin as sin. He may indeed,

First, hate sin in another, but not in himself: thus one proud man hates another.... "Why," says Christ to the hypocrite, "beholdest thou the mote[1] in thy brother's eye, but considerest not the beam that is in thine eye?" (Matt. 7:3). How quick in espying[2] and rash in censuring the smallest fault in another is the hypocrite! It was but one fault, and that but a small one, but a mote that he could find in another. Yet this he quickly discerns: it may be there were many excellent graces in him; these he overlooks, but the mote he plainly discerns.

It may be that mote in his brother's eye had drawn many tears from it, but these he takes no notice of, and meanwhile there is a beam, a great, horrid, flagitious evil in himself, but it is too near him to be discerned or bewailed. This is a sad symptom of a naughty heart.

Secondly, he may hate it in its effects and consequents, not in its own nature, as the thief hates the

---

From *Touchstone of Sincerity,* in *Works,* 5:554–55.

1. *mote*: speck of dust
2. *espying*: noticing

gallows, not the wickedness that he has done. It is not sin in itself, but sin in its connection with hell that is frightful to him. The unsound professor could wish that there were no such threatenings in the Bible against sin. When sin tempts him, "I would," he says, "but I fear the consequence. O sin, if I could separate you from hell, nothing should separate you and me."

Thirdly, he may hate it in a mood or pang, but not with a rooted, habitual hatred. It's plain from 2 Peter 2:22 that sin may sometimes rest upon the conscience of an unregenerate man as a load lies upon a sick stomach, and so he may discharge himself of it by reformation, restitution, etc., but a little time reconciles the quarrel between him and his lust again. If they fall out they will fall in again; "the dog is turned to his own vomit again; and the sow that was washed to her wallowing in the mire."

35

The Saint's Hatred of Sin

But an upright soul hates sin in another manner, and in this hatred of sin the children of God are manifest.

First, the opposition of sin to God is the very ground and formal reason upon which a gracious soul opposes and hates it. If it is opposite to the holy nature and law of God, it must be odious in His eyes. This put David's heart, "Against thee, thee only, have I sinned" (Ps. 51:4). "I have wronged Uriah greatly. I have wronged myself and family greatly; but the wrong I have done to others is not worth naming in comparison of the wrong I have done to Thee."

Secondly, the upright soul hates sin in himself more than he hates it in any other, as a man hates a serpent in the hedge, but much more in his own bosom: "But I see another law in my members...I find then a law, that, when I would do good, evil is present with me" (Rom. 7:23, 21). I don't know how others find it, but I am sure I find sin in my very bosom, in my very bowels; it is present with me. O wretched man that I am! A gracious soul can mourn to see in others, but to find it in himself pierces him to the very heart.

Thirdly, the gracious soul hates not only this or that particular sin, but the whole kind—everything

---

From *Touchstone of Sincerity*, in *Works*, 5:555–56.

that is sinful. True hatred is of the whole nature or kind. "I hate every false way" (Ps. 119:104), sins that are profitable and pleasant as well as sins that have neither profit nor pleasure; sins that are secret as well as sins that are open and will defame him....

Fourthly, the sincere soul hates sin with an irreconcilable hatred. There was a time when sin and his soul fell out, but there never will be a time of reconciliation between them again. That breach that effectual conviction once made can never be made up any more: they will return no more to folly (Ps. 85:8). Indeed, it seems to those who have suffered so much for sin, who have endured so many fears and sorrows for it, the greatest folly in the world is to return to sin again: no, no, they admire the mercy of their escape from sin to their dying day and never look back upon their former state but with shame and grief....

Fifthly, the sincere soul hates sin with a superlative hatred. He hates it more than any other evil in the world besides it....

Sixthly, to conclude, so deep is the hatred that upright ones bear to sin that nothing pleases them more than the thoughts of a full deliverance from it: "I thank God through Jesus Christ our Lord" (Rom. 7:25). What does he so heartily thank God for? O for a prospect of his final deliverance from sin, never to be entangled, defiled, or troubled with it anymore. And this is one thing that sweetens death to the saints as much as anything in the world can do, except Christ's victory over it and lying in the grave for us. To think of a grave is not pleasant in itself, but to think of a parting time with sin, that's sweet and pleasant indeed.

36

The Hypocrite's Sorrow for Sin

Also, merely feeling troubled for your sin does not argue for sincerity of repentance. Some have reason to be troubled even for their troubles for sin. So have they,

First, those who are troubled only for the commission of some more gross sins that startle the natural conscience, but not for inward sins that defile the soul. Judas was troubled for betraying innocent blood, but not for that base lust of covetousness that was the root of it or the want of sincere love to Jesus Christ (Matt. 27:4–5). Outward sins are sins *majoris infamiae*, of greatest scandal; but heart sins are oftentimes *majoris reatus*, sins of greater guilt. To be troubled for grosser sins and have no trouble for ordinary sins daily incurred is an ill sign of a bad heart.

Secondly, a graceless heart may be much troubled at the discovery of sin when it is not troubled for the guilt of sin. "As the thief is ashamed when he is found, so is the house of Israel ashamed" (Jer. 2:26). Hence it is that they try not to commit ten sins against God in order to hide one sin from the eyes of men. It is a mercy that sin is the matter of men's shame, and that all are not arrived to that height of impudence to declare their sin as Sodom and glory

From *Touchstone of Sincerity,* in *Works,* 5:556–57.

in their shame. But to be ashamed only because men see it, and not with Ezra to say, "O my God, I am ashamed, and blush to lift up my face to thee," that is, ashamed that Thou seest it, is but hypocrisy (Ezra 9:6).

Thirdly, a graceless heart may be troubled for the rod that sin draws after it, but not for sin itself, as it provokes God to inflict such rods.

37

The Saint's Sorrow for Sin

But the troubles of upright ones for sin are of another kind and nature.

First, they are troubled that God is wrong and His Spirit troubled by their sins. So the penitent prodigal says, "I have sinned against heaven, and in thy sight" (Luke 15:21): against heaven, that is, against Him whose throne is in heaven, a great, glorious, and infinite majesty. A poor worm of the earth has lifted up his hand against the God of heaven.

Secondly, they are troubled for the defilement of their own souls by sin; hence they are compared in Proverbs 25:26 to a troubled fountain. You know it's the property of a living spring when any filth falls into it, or that which lies in the bottom of its channel is raised and defiles its streams, never to leave working till it has purged itself of it and recovered its purity again.

So it is with a righteous man. He loves purity in the precept (Ps. 119:140), and he loves it no less in the principles and practice. He thinks it is hell enough to lie under the pollution of sin, if he should ever come under damnation for it.

Thirdly, they are troubled for the estrangements of God and the hiding of His face from them because

From *Touchstone of Sincerity,* in *Works,* 5:557–58.

of their sin. It would go close to an ingenuous spirit to see a dear and faithful friend whom he has grieved look strangely and shyly upon him at the next meeting, as if he did not know him. Much more does it go to the heart of a gracious man to see the face of God turned from him, and not to be toward him as in times past. This is how David's heart went after his fall, as you may see: "Cast me not away from thy presence, and take not thy holy spirit from me" (Ps. 51:11). Lord, if Thou turn Thy back upon me and estrange Thyself from me, I am a lost man. That is the greatest mischief that can befall me.

Fourthly, their troubles for sin run deep to what other men's do. They are strong to bear other troubles, but quail[1] and faint under this (Ps. 38:4). Other sorrows may for the present be violent and make more noise, but this sorrow soaks deeper into the soul.

Fifthly, their troubles for sin are more private and silent troubles than others are. Their sore runs in the night, as it is in Psalm 77:2. Not but that they may and do open their troubles to men (and it is a mercy when they meet with a judicious, tender, and experienced Christian to unbosom themselves unto), but when all is done it is God and your soul alone that must whisper out the matter. That is a sincere sorrow for sin indeed, which is expressed secretly to God in the closet.

Sixthly, their troubles are incurable by creature comforts. It is not the removing some outward pressures and inconveniencies that can remove their

---

1. *quail*: falter

Aurelius Augustine (354–430)

Augustine was perhaps the most influential
theologian from the early church whose works
greatly influenced the Reformed tradition.

burden. Nothing but pardon, peace, and witnessed reconciliation can quiet the gracious heart.

Seventhly, their troubles for sin are ordered and kept in their own place. They dare not stamp the dignity of Christ's blood upon their worthless tears and groans for sin.... "Lord, wash my sinful tears in the blood of Christ" was once the desire of a true penitent. And thus our trouble for sin shows us what our hearts are.[2]

---

2. Flavel referenced Augustine (354–430), bishop and Latin theologian, who was bishop of Hippo, which is present-day Annaba, Algeria.

38

The Saint's Struggle with Sin

But whatever surprises or captivities to sin may befall an upright soul, yet it appears by these eight following particulars that he is not the servant of sin or in full subjection to it. For,

First, though he may be drawn to sin, yet he cannot reflect upon his sin without shame and sorrow, which plainly shows it to be an involuntary surprise. So Peter wept bitterly (Matt. 26:75), and David mourned for his sin heartily. Others can fetch new pleasures out of their old sins by reflecting on them, and some can glory in their shame (Phil. 3:19). Some are stupid and senseless after sin, and the sorrow of a carnal heart for it is but a morning dew; but it is far otherwise with God's people.

Secondly, though a saint may be drawn to sin, yet it is not with a deliberate and full consent of his will. Their delight is in the law of God (Rom. 7:16, 22). There are inward dislikes from the new nature, and as for that case of David, which seems to have so much of counsel and deliberation in it, yet it was but a single act. It was not in the general course of his life. He was upright in all things in the general course and tenor of his life (1 Kings 15:5).

From *Touchstone of Sincerity,* in *Works,* 5:561–63.

Thirdly, though an upright soul may fall into sin, yet he is restless and unquiet in that condition, like a bone out of joint, and that shows he is not one of sin's servants. As on the contrary, if a man is engaged in the external duties of religion and is restless and unquiet there, his heart is not in it. He is not at rest until he is again in his earthly business; this man cannot be reckoned Christ's servant. A gracious heart is much after that rate employed in the work of sin than a carnal heart is employed in the work of religion....

Fourthly, though a sincere Christian falls into sin and commits evil, yet he proceeds not from evil to evil as the ungodly do (Jer. 9:3) but makes his fall into one sin a caution to prevent another sin.... It is not so with the servants of sin. One sin leaves them much more disposed to another sin.

Fifthly, a sincere Christian may be drawn to sin, yet he would be glad with all his heart to be rid of sin. It would be more to him than thousands of gold and silver, that he might grieve and offend God no more; and that shows sin is not in dominion over him. He that is under the dominion of sin is loath to leave his lusts....

Sixthly, it appears they yield not themselves willingly to obey sin, in as much as it is the matter of their joy when God orders any providence to prevent sin in them. "Blessed be the LORD..." says David to Abigail, "and blessed be thy advice, and blessed be thou, which hast kept me this day from coming to shed blood" (1 Sam. 25:32–33)....

Seventhly, this shows that some who may be drawn to commit sin yet are none of the servants of sin, because they do heartily beg the assistance of grace to keep them from sin: "Keep back thy servant also from presumptuous sins," says the psalmist, "let them not have dominion over me" (Ps. 19:13). Lord, I find propensities to sin in my nature. Yea, and strong ones too if Thou leave me to myself. I am carried into sin as easily as a feather down the torrent. "O, Lord, keep back thy servant." And there is no petition that upright ones pour out their hearts to God in, either more frequently or more ardently than in this, to be kept back from sin.

Eighthly, and lastly, this shows the soul not to be under the dominion of sin, because it does not only cry to God to be kept back from sin, but it also uses the means of prevention himself. He resists it, as well as prays against it (Ps. 18:23; Job 31:1; Isa. 33:15). See with what care the portals that sin uses to enter are shut.

39

Wrongly Censuring Your Heart

You see of what importance the duty of self-examination is, how many things put a necessity and a solemnity upon that work. Now in the close of all, I would offer you some helps for the due management thereof. That is as far as I can carry it. The Lord persuade your hearts to the diligent and faithful application and use of them. The general rules to clear sincerity are these that follow.

Rule 1. We may not presently conclude we are in the state of hypocrisy because we find some working of it and tendencies to it in our spirits. The best gold has some dross and alloy in it. Hypocrisy is a weed naturally springing in the ground. The best heart is not perfectly clear free of it....

Rule 2. Every true ground of humiliation for sin is not a sufficient ground for doubting and questioning our estate and condition. There are many more things to humble us upon the account of our infirmity than there are to stumble us upon the account of our integrity. It is the sin and affliction of some poor souls to call their condition in question upon every slip and failing in the course of their obedience. This is the way to debar ourselves from all

From *Touchstone of Sincerity,* in *Works,* 5:595–98.

the peace and comfort of the Christian life.... Be as severe to yourselves as you will, always provided you be just: "There is that maketh himself rich, yet hath nothing: there is that maketh himself poor, yet hath great riches" (Prov. 13:7).... It is but an ill requital, an ungrateful return to God for the best of mercies, to undervalue them in our hearts and be ready upon all occasions to put them away as worth nothing.

Rule 3. A stronger propensity in our nature and more frequent incidence in our practice to one sin than another does not presently infer our hypocrisy and the unsoundness of our hearts in religion. It is true, every hypocrite has some way of wickedness: some *peccatum in deliciis*, iniquity that he delights in and rolls as a sweet morsel under his tongue, some lust that he is not willing to part with nor can endure that the knife of mortification should touch it, and this undoubtedly argues the insincerity and rottenness of his heart. And it is true also, that the nature and constitution of the most sanctified man inclines him rather to one sin than to another, though he allow himself in none. Yea, though he set himself more watchfully against that sin than another, yet he may still have more trouble and vexation, more temptation and defilement from it than any other.

Rule 4. A great backwardness and indisposition to one duty rather than another does not conclude the heart to be unsound and false with God, provided we do not inwardly dislike and disapprove any duty of religion or except against it in our agreement with Christ, but that it rises merely from the present weakness and distemper we labor under.

There are some duties in religion, such as sufferings for Christ, bearing sharp reproofs for sin, etc., that even an upright heart, under a present distemper, may find a great deal of backwardness and loathness to; yet still he consents to the law that it is good, is troubled that he cannot comply more cheerfully with his duty, and desires to stand complete in all the will of God. Perfection is his aim, and imperfections are his sorrows.

Rule 5. The glances of the eye at self-ends in duties— while self is not the weight that moves the wheels, the principal end and design we drive at, and while those glances are corrected and mourned for—do not conclude the heart to be unsound and hypocritical in religion. For even among the most deeply sanctified, few can keep their eye so steady and fixed with pure and unmixed respects to the glory of God, but that there will be (alas, too frequently) some by-ends insinuating and creeping into the heart.

Rule 6. The doubts and fears that hang upon and perplex our spirits about the hypocrisy of our hearts do not conclude that therefore we are what we fear ourselves to be. God will not condemn every one for a hypocrite that suspects, yea, or charges himself with hypocrisy....

40

━━━ ⊷ «(•)» ⊶ ━━━

Questions to Judge Sincerity

Well, then, let not the upright be unjust to themselves in censuring their own heart. They are bad enough, but let us not make them worse than they are but thankfully own and acknowledge the least degrees of grace and integrity in them. And possibly our uprightness might be sooner discovered to us if, in a due composure of spirit, we would sit down and attend the true answers of our own hearts to such questions as these.

Question 1: Do I make the approbation of God or the applause of men the very end and main design of my religious performances, accord to 1 Thessalonians 2:4 and Colossians 3:23? Will the acceptation of my duties with men satisfy me, whether God accepts my duties and person or not?

Question 2: Is it the reproach and shame that attends sin at present and the danger and misery that will follow it hereafter that restrains me from the commission of it? Or is it the fear of God in my soul and the hatred I bear to sin as it is sin, according to Psalm 19:12 and 119:113?

From *Touchstone of Sincerity,* in *Works,* 5:598–99.

Question 3: Can I truly and heartily rejoice to see God's work carried on in the world and His glory promoted by other hands, though I have no share in the credit and honor of it, as Paul did (Phil. 1:18)?

Question 4: Is there no duty in religion so full of difficulty and self-denial, but I desire to comply with it? And is all the holy and good will of God acceptable to my soul, though I cannot rise up with like readiness to the performance of all duties according to that pattern (Ps. 119:6)?

Question 5: Am I sincerely resolved to follow Christ and holiness at all seasons, however the aspects of the times may be upon religion? Or do I bear myself so warily and covertly as to shun all hazards for religion, having a secret reserve in my heart to launch out no farther than I may return with safety, contrary to the practice and resolution of upright souls (Pss. 116:3; 44:18–19; Rev. 22:11)?

Question 6: Do I make no conscience of committing secret sins or neglecting secret duties? Or am I conscientious both in the one and other according to the rules and patterns of integrity (Matt. 6:5–6; Ps. 19:12)?

A few such questions solemnly propounded to our own hearts, in a calm and serious hour, would find them and discover much of their sincerity toward the Lord.

41

Deep Trials of the Heart

My friends, the Lord Jesus has set down the terms, and He will not come lower, and if you cannot come up to His terms, Christ and you must part. He will not come down for the sake of any man; therefore consider those things. Now, he that is contented to part with all, rather than part with Christ, that soul is for Christ, and Christ is for that soul. But there is the last thing, and that is the embracing of all those things that may help you to enjoy Christ: these are deep trials of the heart, and therefore it concerns us to make deep searches here. Well, then, there are four things that do further a man's soul in the way to Christ, and are you contented, and that deliberately, Christians, to embrace them all to help you to Christ?

1. First, are you contented to embrace and welcome all the ordinances of God and duties of religion, both public and private, without exception of one of them? Can you turn your feet to all His ordinances?... If you are Christ's, you must come under the law of His house.

From James Burdwood, *Helps for Faith and Patience in Times of Affliction...to Which Is Also Added, A Sure Tryal of a Christian's State, by John Flavell, Late Minister (also) in Dartmouth* (London, 1693), 273–75.

2. Secondly, are you contented to embrace all fatherly corrections from the hand of God for the killing of the remainders of sin in you? If you will be for Christ, you must submit to Christ's method: It is in vain to say, "If I can travel to heaven without meeting a storm in the way, I am willing to go"; you must be contented with all afflictions to enter into the kingdom of heaven. Paul could say, in 2 Corinthians 12:10, "Therefore I take pleasure in infirmities…in persecutions…for Christ's sake: for when I am weak, then am I strong."

3. Thirdly, if you will be Christ's, you must submit to all those means Christ has appointed for the mortification of your corruptions, be they never so hard: rebukes from God, rebukes from men, by afflictions, and by the Word, for the mortification of sin. Can you say, Christians, that you are willing to have your mistakes directed by God or men, your corruptions discovered, anything that helps to the pulling up the roots of corruption? Surely thus it must be if you will be for Christ, all faithful admonitions, all necessary afflictions.

4. Fourthly, and lastly, if you will be for Christ, and be His, you must embrace all pains, watchings, and laborings after holiness to the end of your days: holiness will cost a Christian abundance of labor, but this you must do, or you cannot be Christians. "Having these promises, dearly beloved, let us cleanse ourselves from all filthiness of the flesh and spirit, perfecting holiness in the fear of God" (2 Cor. 7:1). Here's the work of a Christian, cleansing work, and perfecting work in the fear of God, to the end of

our lives.... He that is contented with these terms is surely Christ's as ever was any soul.

CONCLUSION

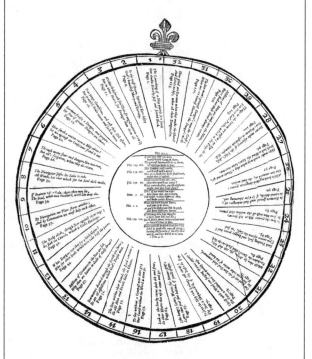

Table of Contents to
Navigation Spiritualized: A New Compass for Sea-men

Flavel used ordinary objects related to boats to convey
spiritual truths to the sailors in his community.

42

A Blessed End

To conclude, God will shortly put a blessed end to all these troubles, cares, and watchings. The time is coming when your heart will be as you would have it, when you will be discharged of these cares, fears, and sorrows and never cry out, "Oh my hard, my proud, my vain, my earthly heart" anymore: when all darkness will be banished from your understanding, and you will clearly discover all truths in God, that crystal ocean of truth; when all vanity will be purged perfectly out of your thoughts, and they will be everlastingly, ravishingly, and delightfully entertained and exercised upon that supreme goodness and infinite excellency of God, from whom they shall never start anymore like a broken bow. And as for your pride, passion, earthliness, and all other matters of your complaint and trouble, it shall be said of them, as of [Moses] to Israel, "Stand still, and see the salvation of the LORD" (Ex. 14:13).[1] These corruptions you see today, henceforth you shall see them no more forever, when you shall lay down your weapons of prayers, tears, and groans and put on the armor of light, not to fight but to triumph in.

Lord, when shall this blessed day come? How long? How long? Holy and true; my soul waits for Thee....

From *A Saint Indeed*, in *Works*, 5:508–9.

1. Flavel's work mistakenly reads "Egyptians" instead of "Moses."

Archibald Alexander (1772–1851)

Alexander attributed much spiritual benefit to
Flavel's works, saying "To John Flavel I certainly
owe more than to any uninspired author."

Reading Flavel

The first collection of Flavel's works was printed in 1701, with numerous reprints following throughout the eighteenth and nineteenth centuries. The latest reprint, from 1820, is found in the Banner of Truth Trust's six-volume edition of Flavel's works.[1] The Banner edition contains thirty-six titles, including appendices. Joel Beeke and Randall Pederson suggest, "If you can afford only a few sets of Puritan works, Flavel's should be included."[2]

So where does one begin reading in Flavel's works? Though some of his writings were polemical, most contain practical expositions and sermons filled with devotional material. Here is a suggested reading plan. The volume that includes the specific title in the Banner of Truth Trust edition is cited in parentheses.[3]

---

1. John Flavel, *The Works of John Flavel*, 6 vols. (1820; repr., Edinburgh: Banner of Truth, 1997).

2. Joel R. Beeke and Randall J. Pederson, *Meet the Puritans, with a Guide to Modern Reprints* (Grand Rapids: Reformation Heritage Books, 2006), 252.

3. For Beeke and Pederson's extended overview of all six volumes of Flavel's works, see *Meet the Puritans*, 250–52.

Shorter, Practical Works

Begin by reading Flavel's shorter, practical works. Besides the two works contained in this book that primarily focus on the heart,[4] start with Flavel's popular *Divine Conduct, or The Mystery of Providence* (vol. 4), a treatise on Psalm 57:2.[5] Flavel shows us how to find God's involvement in every aspect of the world and our life. Sinclair Ferguson states that this work "stands out for its insightful, biblical and pastorally sensitive realism. Here is truly a Puritan and spiritual classic."[6] There are other short treatises worth reading before moving on to his sermons. Read *A Practical Treatise of Fear* (vol. 3), an exposition on Isaiah 8:12–13, which focuses on how the godly control their fear of man and rightly fear God instead.[7] Printed in 1682, this work was originally published alongside *The Righteous Man's Refuge* (vol. 3), an exposition on Isaiah 26:20, which

---

4. Both *Keeping the Heart* (called *A Saint Indeed*) and *Signs of Grace* (called *The Touchstone of Sincerity*) are in volume 5 of the Banner edition.

5. This book is also available in paperback as *The Mystery of Providence* (Edinburgh: Banner of Truth, 1963).

6. Sinclair B. Ferguson, "The Mystery of Providence by John Flavel," in *The Devoted Life: An Invitation to the Puritan Classics*, ed. Kelly M. Kapic and Randall C. Gleason (Downers Grove, Ill.: IVP, 2004), 211. Also see John J. Murray, "John Flavel and the Problem of Providence," in *Triumph through Tribulation: Papers Read at the 1998 Westminster Conference* (Stoke-on-Trent, U.K.: Tentmaker Publications, 1998), 99–118, and Mark Deckard, "Why Is This Happening to Me? The Mystery of Providence," in *Helpful Truth in Past Places: The Puritan Practice of Biblical Counseling* (Ross-shire: Christian Focus, 2009), 17–46.

7. This book has been recently republished as *Triumphing over Sinful Fear* (Grand Rapids: Reformation Heritage Books, 2011).

instructs Christians on finding refuge in God's attributes during times of persecution.[8] Gerald Cragg summarizes the significance that Puritans placed on God's attributes and persecution: "The consideration of God's attributes led naturally to the experience of God's presence. The sense of God's nearness was a support in 'opposing tribunals' or in prisons; there was no affliction that need shake the firm assurance that God was near at hand."[9] Related to the theme of suffering is another small treatise, *Preparation for Suffering* (vol. 6). This work offers a thorough explanation of how the Spirit prepares believers to suffer for the gospel's sake as did Paul in Acts 21:13. It contains some of Flavel's best material on saving and sanctifying grace. Particularly stirring is Flavel's treatise on dealing with the death of a child in *A Token for Mourners* (vol. 5).[10] The resulting sorrow is inevitable and intense, but it must be understood in light of God's purposes, and it must not be excessive. Finally, *The Reasonableness of Personal Conversion and the Necessity of Conversion* (vol. 6), as the title suggests, encourages nonbelievers to see the necessity of turning from their sins and worshiping Christ.

---

8. John Flavel, *Two Treatises, the First of Fear, from Isa. 8, v. 12, 13, and Part of 14; the Second, The Righteous Man's Refuge in the Evil Day, from Isaiah 26, verse 20* (London, 1682).

9. Gerald R. Cragg, *Puritanism in the Period of the Great Persecution, 1660–1688* (Cambridge: Cambridge University Press, 1957), 84.

10. This work was recently published as *Facing Grief: Counsel for Mourners* (Edinburgh: Banner of Truth, 2009).

Sermons

Next, read Flavel's sermons, which were usually collected into large volumes.[11] Several of the selections
in this book came from *England's Duty* (vol. 4), a collection of sermons from Revelation 3:20 published
near the end of his ministry that God used to convert
many in Dartmouth.[12] These sermons demonstrate
Christ's patience and power in drawing sinners to
Himself. Flavel labeled two of his collected volumes
of sermons his "Doctrine of Christ."[13] The first
of these volumes contains forty-two christological
sermons called *The Fountain of Life* (vol. 1). In his
extensive work on Christian preaching, Hughes Oliphant Old comments on this work, "One might say it
is not so much a systematic Christology as an exposi-
tory Christology. It is not a speculative Christology; it
is both practical and profound."[14] The second volume,
The Method of Grace (vol. 2), contains thirty-five sermons on how the Spirit applies Christ's redemptive
work to the elect. In this work, Flavel's sermon *The
Loveliness of Christ* (sermon 12) is his most affectionate
and stirring meditation on Jesus in all of his writings.

---

11. Banner of Truth has republished several of Flavel's sermons
in its Pocket Puritan series: *Impure Lust* (2008), *Binge Drinking* (2008),
and *Sinful Speech* (2009).

12. *Life of Flavel, Whole Works*, I:[iv]. Revelation 3:20 reads,
"Behold, I stand at the door and knock: if any man hear my voice,
and open the door, I will come in to him, and will sup with him,
and he with me."

13. John Flavel, *Pneumatologia, A Treatise of the Soul of Man*
(London, 1685), [xviii].

14. Hughes Oliphant Old, *The Reading and Preaching of the
Scriptures in the Worship of the Christian Church, Vol. 4: The Age of the
Reformation* (Grand Rapids: Eerdmans, 2002), 318.

After these two volumes, read Flavel's sermons on the human soul contained in *The Soul of Man* (vols. 2–3). He pays particular interest to the soul's creation in the image of God and how to prepare for death. Finally, his twelve sermons on the Lord's Supper, *Twelve Sacramental Meditations* (vol. 6), prepares communicants for fellowship with Christ at the table. Connected to these sermons is a conversation between a minister and a church member who are wondering if they should partake of the Supper (vol. 6). There are also individual sermons scattered throughout his works dealing with issues such as church unity (vol. 3), religious liberty (vol. 3), the coronation of William of Orange (vol. 6), a funeral sermon along with an exposition on covenant theology from 2 Samuel 23:5 (vol. 6), and a sermon on what Christ says are the qualifications for gospel ministry (vol. 6).

Creative Writings

Before delving into Flavel's doctrinal material, take time exploring some of his more creative writing. Flavel lived in the naval city of Dartmouth and then, because of the Five Mile Act, resided among the gardens and farms of Slapton, and these circumstances offered him a chance to produce two of his most imaginative works, *Navigation Spiritualized* (vol. 5) and *Husbandry Spiritualized* (vol. 5). In these works he takes ordinary objects related to sailing and farming and draws out spiritual application, most often in poetic form. Also, he records an experience of God's deliverance from a sea storm in *A Narrative of Some Late and Wonderful Sea Deliverances* (vol. 4). Finally, there are two works devoted to how Dartmouth's sailors could fight sin in *A Caution to Seamen* (vol. 5) and *The Seamen's Companion* (vol. 5).

Doctrinal Writings

Conclude by reading Flavel's doctrinal writings. The first, and most devotional, is his exposition on the Westminster Assembly's Shorter Catechism (vol. 6). He used the question-and-answer format to instruct young and old alike throughout his ministry. This work is particularly helpful because each question contains "inferences," where he draws out practical advice on how to live out the doctrine he teaches. Two short treatises, *A Serious and Seasonable Caveat* (vol. 4) and *Tidings from Rome* (vol. 4), focus on the dangers of Roman Catholicism. Doctrinal error, Flavel contends in *The Causes and Remedies of Mental Errors* (vol. 3), begins with misappropriating Scripture and logic. As one who believed in infant baptism, Flavel disputed with the Baptist Philip Cary on the relationship between the covenants and its implication on who should be baptized (see *A Reply to Mr. Philip Cary's Solemn Call* in volume 6 and a further reply in volume 3:493–550). In addition, Flavel wrote against the implications of antinomian doctrine in *A Brief Account of the Rise and Growth of Antinomianism* (vol. 3). Not found in the Banner edition is Flavel's correspondence with a local Quaker and friend, Clement Lake.[15] These letters reveal Flavel's love for his friend, but also the

---

15. *Flavel, the Quaker and the Crown: John Flavel, Clement Lake, and Religious Liberty in 17th Century England* (repr., Cambridge: Rhwymbooks, 2000).

strength of his doctrinal convictions relating to the Spirit's relationship to Scripture. Attached to these letters is John Galpine's short "Life of John Flavel." James Burdwood's reprinted sermon from Flavel has not been reprinted since the 1600s.

Yea, more than so, we triumph now
In God with one accord,
Having receiv'd atonement through
Christ Jesus our own Lord.

Wherefore to Him, who is the first
Begotten of the dead,
Who over earthly princes must
Be supreme Lord and Head:

Ev'n unto Him who lov'd us so,
To wash us in His blood,
And make us kings and priests unto
His Father and His God:

To Him dominion therefore,
By us be given, when
This present world shall be no more;
To which we say, amen.[16]

---

16. *The Whole Works of the Reverend Mr. John Flavel, Late Minister at Dartmouth in Devon, in Two Volumes* (London, 1701), 2:696. This hymn can be sung to the tunes of the well-known hymns "Amazing Grace" and "O God, Our Help in Ages Past."

A Hymn upon Romans 5:6–11

When we were destitute of strength,
Ourselves to help or save,
Christ for ungodliness at length
His life a ransom gave.

For one that's righteous, we would grudge
To lay our life at stake;
And for a good man, it were much
Such an exchange to make.

But God His matchless love commends,
In that Christ Jesus dies
For us, when we were not His friends,
But wretched enemies.

Much more, being justify'd and free
Thro' His own blood, from sin;
From wrath to come we sav'd shall be,
Ev'n by the life of Him.

For if, when enemies, for us
Christ's death did end the strife;
Much more, when reconciled thus,
He'll save us by His life.